The (Don't Have) To Do List

With Our Strongest Love.

Pat & Fred Wood

The (Don't Have) To Do List

Enjoying a Stress Free Life

Anthony Delaney

New Wine Press

New Wine Ministries
PO Box 17
Chichester
West Sussex
United Kingdom
PO20 6YB

Scripture quotations are taken from the following versions of the Bible:

NIV – The Holy Bible, New International Version. Copyright © 1973, 1978, 1984 by International Bible Society. Used by permission.

NKJV – The Holy Bible, New King James Version. Copyright © 1982 by Thomas Nelson Inc.

The Message – Copyright © 1993, 1994, 1995, 1996, 2000, 2001, 2002 by Eugene H. Peterson

CEV – Contemporary English Version. Copyright © 1995 by American Bible Society

GNB – Good News Bible. Copyright © 1994 by the Bible Societies/ HarperCollins Publishers Ltd. Used with permission.

LB – The Living Bible. Copyright © 1971 Tyndale House Publishers.

ISBN 1–903725–56–9

Typeset by CRB Associates, Reepham, Norfolk
Cover design by CCD, www.ccdgroup.co.uk
Printed in Malta

About the Author

Anthony Delaney is ordained in the Church of England and leads an exciting and fast growing church in West Horsley, Surrey, England. If you want to find out more about his church watch the video at www.l1fe.org

Raised in Manchester, Anthony left school and joined the police cadets at sixteen years of age before qualifying as a Police Officer with Greater Manchester Police. He worked a tough inner city beat for ten years exemplary service in total, where he received two Chief Constable's commendations for bravery.

Following a dramatic experience of meeting Jesus – not on the road to Damascus but the road through Gorton – he became a follower of Christ at the age of twenty-one.

Anthony sought to bring his new found spiritual principles to bear in his work life. His passion to tell others the great news that changed his own life led him to working in a voluntary capacity with young people, with whom he still has a great ability to relate.

He left the police force to train for ministry, gaining an honours degree in Theology. He has ministered in large churches in Devon and Kent, before the move to Surrey in 2001.

Using practical wisdom, ready humour and real-life experience of life's ups and downs, Anthony is much in demand as an inspirational speaker. He also consults with churches and businesses (public and private sector) in leadership and organisational strategy, helping individuals and organisations achieve their potential and true success and satisfaction.

Following God's plan for his life has led him to Africa, the USA and Canada to speak, as well as leading outreach events in towns and cities in almost every region of the UK.

In his spare time he trains for marathons and more recently triathlons. He firmly believes that following God's leading is the only way to real joy in life, and that as we hear his voice, heed his words and speak his truth, we receive the best possible life.

Married to Zoë, who works in the field of ophthalmic medicine, he is the proud Dad of Emma, Hannah and Joel.

What others are saying about *The (Don't Have) To Do List* and Anthony Delaney

"Beware! Buying this book could be dangerous to your self-image – that is if you live behind a mask, are governed by the fear of what others think, or are afraid to get it wrong. Ant Delaney is one of those rare things – an original. So many people are plastic copies, but he is real. He has dedicated his life to enabling others to break out and become originals themselves. This book will help you do just that. Read it!"

Eric Delve, Area Dean of Maidstone
Six-preacher of Canterbury Cathedral

"It is essential that young men of God rise up to carry on the greatest task given to anyone, the teaching of God's precious, holy Word. To aspire to such a calling is one thing, but to fulfil it is another. As one who loves God's Word and is passionate about the continuing faith of the Church, I am thrilled that men like Anthony Delaney are one of God's chosen vessels. He is surely one of tomorrow's men!"

Dr R.T. Kendall, international speaker and author

"Anthony Delaney writes as he speaks – from God's heart to your heart. Our vicar and family friend during the last three years, I could not recommend his teaching more highly. This book is a must read for all of us wanting to experience the total freedom that comes from a loving and personal relationship with Jesus Christ. It will speak to everyone."

Sarah de Carvalho, author of *The Street Children of Brazil* and founder of Happy Child Mission, Brazil

"Anthony Delaney loves life. There have been times when Anthony and I have been together ministering in Africa when we laughed so much it hurt. This book is incredibly timely. His words connect and bring great freedom. People need to know 'I don't have to please everyone', and 'I don't have to worry if someone rejects me'. Read this for yourself, and give one to a friend."

*Rev. **Andy Economides***, Christian communicator
and founder of Soteria Trust

"Ant has a conviction that God has put far more potential in people's lives than they often seem to achieve. It comes as no surprise to me that he should write a book full of practical common sense and godly advice on living life more effectively. The writer of Proverbs says that plans fail for lack of advice, so read this book, take the advice and then watch what God can do!"

Russ Hughes, Worship Director
St Luke's, Maidstone

Contents

Foreword

Some of us live by lists that can become oppressive and even cause us to be insensitive to those around us. Some of us don't live by lists, and we are often surrounded by people who are convinced we are going to forget this, that and the other because without lists, we cannot live! And then, when those who live without lists do forget, it only confirms the foolishness of living without a list for those who are bound by them.

But lists are a part of life for most of us.

However, Anthony Delaney, who is both fun and funny, has created a different sort of book from any other you would have read before. Only somebody with a slightly quirky mind would have even thought of such a thing. Anthony has a "things I *don't have to do*" list. There is nothing to cross off this list as you will see.

It reminds us of how life could be if we focused on what has been done for us, what has been provided for us, who and what surrounds us, and that we should be shaped by our unseen future, not by our well worn, often over-rehearsed past.

There is good biblical teaching here (come to think of it the Bible has got quite a few lists itself!), but it is liberally peppered with stories to illustrate the important points being made.

I commend Anthony Delaney and this book to you, and I

hope you will be hearing a lot more from him in the years to come. Enjoy the read. And if you have no time now, just put it on a list!

Gerald Coates

Dedication

Henry Gilmore Delaney (1938–2005).
A great Dad.
See you soon.

Preface –
The Ultimate Life Coach

I get fed up telling people I'm a church leader.

Not because I'm ashamed of being a Christian (which is without doubt the best possible life).

Not because I'm ashamed of my church, which numbers some of the most loving, caring, fantastic, talented, fun and interesting people I've ever known.

No, it's not any of that. It's not even because sometimes people want you to wear a collar that looks silly and makes your neck hot!

It's the Vicar image all over.

Leading a church in England, people peg you immediately as a kind of Derek Nimmo character from *All Gas and Gaiters*, complete with buck teeth to hold in the bad breath, wearing socks and sandals and with a love for natural yogurt you make yourself.

It's not really me (I don't like yogurt). So I usually pretend to be normal instead. I've found people prefer that, which is an encouragement to me.

Recently I went with the wonderful Zoë to consider switching to a different, less expensive gym than the one we now go to in order to hone our already magnificently chiselled bodies. As part of the form-filling the lady with the pen asked Zoë what she did.

"I'm a nurse – a Sister." Not an eyebrow raised.

The young lady looked at me. Until now she had treated me like a normal man. I knew how easily all this could change.

If I just came out with the legal title and said, "Rector", she could have thought I'd got to the medical declaration part of the form too soon (nobody knows what that means).

"Vicar" isn't much better. It brings one of these reactions:

She'd either be telling me about her postcard collection of interesting cathedral spires or she'd blank me totally with a nervous smile like I shouldn't really be allowed in the pool and wonder why I wasn't at home watching pre-recorded videos of *Songs of Praise* over and over.

So I decided to say something different, but true.

"I'm a life coach."

The reaction was overwhelmingly positive. A great big smile.

"Oh, that's so interesting!"

I was amazed. People *never* responded that well when I told them I was a Vicar! I was on a roll. What she said next made it even better.

"So basically, people who are saying, 'Jesus, I need some help with my life' – come to you?"

A glance between Zoë and me.

We both responded together, *"Exactly."*

Hear the claim of the ultimate life coach, Jesus Christ...

> **"I came so they can have real and eternal life,
> more and better life than they ever dreamed of."** [1]

"Better life than you ever dreamed of..." This from the mouth of Jesus Christ, the enigmatic figure who died on a

Roman gibbet 2,000 years ago yet who affected history more than any other person and still commands the allegiance of millions.

He promised those who follow him that they could live the best possible life. It follows that the way of Jesus should therefore be the best possible way for us to live. If not – he's a liar. The choice is that stark. It's either the best possible way for you to live right now in the twenty-first century, or Jesus is a liar. You can test his claims, and if you are a thinking person, you really should.

My son Joel is eleven years old, a purple belt at Karate. When I take him to training I'm always amazed how all the kids line up and are disciplined and do what they're told. It's a complete transformation as they cross the threshold.

The *Sensei* – the teacher – is called Gary. He even looks cool in the white pyjamas. He has nothing to prove, but you know, he exudes a certain air. Don't mess with him. He is the Master.

Recently I sat on the couch and watched a film from the eighties with Joel. He loved it. *The Karate Kid.* If you've seen it you'll remember Mister Miyagi apprentices a young lad and teaches him the ancient Okinawan art. If you've seen the film you'll remember that it was through simple everyday things and repetitions of certain actions that the student learned to become like the master.

Wax on, Wax off.

Paint the Fence.

Sand the Floor.

What is the master the master of? *Karate.* It means "The way of the empty hand". Students who apply themselves to do that, you see a difference in them. Joel is quicker, he's stronger. I don't really want to play fight with him now because it hurts! He's disciplined. He's becoming the type of person you want with you to look after you! Why? Because the teacher is teaching the disciples how to do what he is master of.

What is Jesus Christ the Master of? (Everyone, friend or enemy called him words meaning that – *Rabboni*, Rabbi.) *Jesus is the Master of living.*

He's the ultimate life coach for eternally full life. The ultimate life coach has come to teach us how to live the best possible life; to live in the optimum flow of how God made us to live in this world, and the next.

So if you're a seeker, a sceptic even – and someone handed you this book, try the exercises within it, as chapter by chapter I challenge and invite you to observe the Master of the way of the full life.

Check out the wisdom of this great Eastern teacher and I will help you apply it. See what happens.

If nothing makes any difference, you've lost nothing. If you gain the best possible life from the concepts laid out here, buy another copy and pass it on to someone else!

Anthony Delaney
Sunny Surrey

Introduction

*"People are always getting ready to live,
but never living."*
(Emerson)

My wife Zoë's always telling me to buy a whiteboard. She's a list person, and can't understand why I'm not.

She has a list of people to contact, things to get, dates to fix, and stuff to do. She wants me to do the same, but there's a problem. I'm not very good at lists. They usually make me feel guilty about all the things I *should* be doing, rather then help me focus on what I *am* doing. And she's great at watching the gaps and telling me what I'm forgetting anyway!

So I came up with a different kind of "To Do" list.

I'm told by list lovers that the fun part is when you get to strike off things because you don't have to do them any more. So I just cut to the chase. I found it helped me a great deal and I think it will help you too. You see, since I became a follower of Jesus Christ, the Master of the Full life, I have a "**Things I Don't Have To Do**" list. I can cross lots of things off straight away!

Let me share some of the items on the list with you:

▶ *I don't have to be alone ever again.*
Because God has promised, *"I will never leave you nor forsake you."* [2] No matter where I go or what happens, I can be aware of his love and presence with me always.

▶ *I don't have to be afraid to make commitments any more.*
Because God has made 7,000 promises to me in the Bible, and he keeps his promises, I can make promises to people I love and I know he will help me to keep them.

▶ *I don't have to please everyone.*
The Bible says that if I try to please everyone, I *won't* be able to please God! Doesn't it make a lot of sense to focus on pleasing one person rather than thirty?

▶ *I don't have to worry if someone rejects me.*
I don't have to have everyone's love or approval. Jesus was followed by thousands, but ended up dying on a cross. The apostle Paul was cheered by a crowd who wanted to make him a god in the morning, but by afternoon stoned him till he was almost dead! We can expect to go through some rejection too. It comes with the territory, but I know my heavenly Father will never reject me.

▶ *I don't have to feel guilty any more.*
Not because I haven't done anything wrong or because I try to be a good person (I lost my chance at perfection some way back). Simply because Jesus died for my sins and I have asked for

forgiveness, the Bible says I am washed clean, accepted, adopted into God's family I will not be condemned. So why should I feel guilty? My conscience is clear.

▶ *I don't have to pretend to be in control of everything.*
Left to myself, I could be a bit of a control freak. But God hasn't left me to myself. He's helping me hand over the things I can't control, because the Bible says, *"casting all your care upon Him, for He cares for you".*[3]

That's not all!

- I *don't* have to put on a mask and pretend to be someone I'm not.
- I *don't* have to lose my temper.
- I *don't* have to have it all.
- I *don't* have to be scared of death.
- I *don't* have to have all the answers.
- I *don't* have to meet everyone else's needs.

And I don't have to write a book going into more detail about what some of these mean to me and how they can help people slow down, relax and enjoy more of what the ultimate life coach Jesus, called, "Life in all its fullness".

But I did anyway.

I Don't Have to Be Afraid of Commitments

"He was a self-made man who owed his lack of success to nobody."
(Joseph Heller, *Catch-22*)

I've said I don't "do" to do lists, but I *do* have a list of things I don't have to do any more, since I started living in the way of the Master – Jesus Christ. The first thing you need to know is that I don't have to be afraid of commitments. The fact is, the life I'm excited to experience *starts* with a commitment, but it's not ours. As I look back on the changes that have taken place in my life, it is not so much that, "I prayed a prayer of commitment" (though I did at the age of twenty-one and do again pretty much every day).

No, this started way before that with another commitment, a commitment from God who sent his Son to die for our sins. That happened in harmony with the commitment of God's Son Jesus to hang on a blood stained cross. This awe-inspiring commitment saves me from death, judgment and hell. It overcomes my guilt, it empowers me to live life to the full right now. One day I'll find it is the means by which I get to share eternity with him, reigning with him!

I don't know exactly when Jesus became aware of it in his humanity. I do know it was in the heart of God before the foundation of the world. The plan of "Godislove" meant at the age of thirty-three, as the lambs were being slaughtered during the feast of Passover, Jesus would be betrayed, and suffer for me.

God is committed. He's put himself on oath, because there was nothing greater to swear by than himself. He *will* love me, care for me, forgive, guide and bless me. He didn't have to do any of that, but he did. He does. For you too. Because he's committed to blessing me, I don't have to be afraid of making commitments.

My lack of a daily "To Do" list doesn't mean that I don't have any *goals*. It doesn't mean I'm advocating or encouraging an aimless life.

If anything, you'll soon see that I'm very clear on how vital it is to have goals. (You'll have to want to make and take the time to read this book to benefit from it – set that as a goal for the next little while.) Praying through, discovering and applying some God honouring, challenging goals is going to make all the difference to you, in this life and the next! It's what sets us apart from everything else God made.

God sized goal setting

Let's take a look at what this might mean. I'll ask a few personal questions. (I hope we're getting to know each other well enough to do that without you being too offended.)

- *What are some specific, clear goals about your future that you're committed to?*
- *Have you ever taken time to write such goals out?* If so, you're in a club consisting of only about 3% of people alive right now!

This is really important. Without some direction for the future, you're headed roughly nowhere, however fast you're travelling. You are what one man called "a wandering generality rather than a meaningful specific".[4]

Setting goals

I have goals. Big, challenging goals. Some long-term, some short-term. Some for ministry, some for the church I lead, some for physical fitness, some for spiritual growth, some for continued mental learning, and many for my own personal character traits. One of my goals means that the day after I write this page, I'm going to run the London Marathon.

Some goals I prefer not to share with you – they are known only to God. But a few I will share in broad strokes. I'll just give you some of the words I have written in my journal that I want to be true of me, as the Holy Spirit goes to work day by day. I know I've a long way to go on some of these issues but I want to be, in increasing measure, a man who is . . .

- *Available to others*
- *Appreciative of them*
- *Generous with what I have been given*
- *Faithful to my wife and my word*
- *Pure in heart*
- *A good listener*
- *Inspiring others . . . to believe and live their dreams*
- *A competent and caring leader*
- *Living with nothing to prove*
- *Living with nothing to fear*
- *Living with nothing to hide – as I'm . . .*
- *Headed for heaven*

Did I just say, "A man?" No way! I want to be something far greater than that. I'm a man of God! I want to develop and train others who want to be developed and trained. I want to lead many people to know how intensely fantastic it is to know Jesus Christ. I have goals set about these matters. That's why I'm writing this book. I put it off for years, until I wrote down and dated a goal, and then the book came.

Imagine this – with God on your side, Jesus said, *"**Nothing** will be impossible for you."* [5] So with that promise in mind, where's *your* focus? Have you established some goals for your life? For this year? For this month? Are they written down? Since I put pen to paper on many of my goals I've seen heaven and earth move to get them accomplished.

The Scottish historian and essayist Thomas Carlyle wrote, "a man with half a volition goes back and forth and makes no progress even on the smoothest road, whereas a person with full volition moves ahead steadily no matter how difficult the path".

Many people are like the farmer who shot at the side of his barn and every shot was a bullseye. Finally he admitted it was more bull than eye. He'd painted the targets *after* he'd fired the bullets!

Aim for nothing – and you'll hit it every time. If your goal is to get through today, then go home and watch TV a little before you have to get up tomorrow, you will probably achieve that goal. But God knows there's more to life for you than existing by following the path of least resistance. He wants to unlock the potential he made you with.

Pilgrim's progress

One of my favourite books – I've read it dozens of times – is Bunyan's *Pilgrim's Progress*. Christian reads a book, and discovers in it a life changing truth. The place he's living in and living for is all going to be destroyed! It's the called the City of Destruction, (which should really have been a clue). One day it'll all be gone. So what's the point in only setting goals that will benefit life in that place?

Weighed down and broken hearted by the way he's wasted so much of his life, with a pack on his back full of self-deceit and sin, his despair is only eased when he aligns his heart toward a different goal. He heads out toward the Celestial City. He makes a commitment to walk that way. The kingdom of heaven becomes his driving goal.

I believe the greatest weakness of many people could be summed up as follows:

Even if they have some idea of what it is they want, they have never sat down and counted the cost a commitment would require before it could be brought to completion. Even if they feel it's worth having, they have not made the firm and full decision to pay the price. Without those two steps, success in any venture is unlikely, to say the least.

Jesus was a builder. The word used to describe his pre-Rabbi employment was *teknon*. We could most closely describe him as a stone mason. He knew what he was talking about one day when having a meal at the home of a leading Pharisee.

Picture the scene, the hush descends as Jesus challenges the gathered group about counting the cost of commitments. He's talking here about a commitment to live life for and in God's kingdom. Imagine him now scratching his chin, fixing you with the gaze of any wise builder coming to advise you on a project . . .

> *"Suppose one of you wants to build a tower. What is the first thing you will do? Won't you sit down and figure out how much it will cost and if you have enough money to pay for it? Otherwise, you will start building the tower, but not be able to finish. Then everyone who sees what is happening will laugh at you. They will say, 'You started building, but could not finish the job.'"* [6]

Jesus sounds like a quantity surveyor doesn't he? He challenges people to make sure they have what it takes before they take something on. What caused him to throw down the gauntlet like that? Something another had said a little earlier, at the same meal.

Lying on couches to eat, leaning on the left elbow, maybe the next guy to speak had been having trouble controlling his right elbow and had poured himself too much wine! He shouted out, "Won't it be fantastic when we all get to heaven? What a party that'll be!"

Now I'm sure it will be wonderful, better than we've ever imagined, and I'll talk about that later in the book. But Jesus didn't just agree. He challenged everyone at the party about whether they were really committed to living the heaven-focused life. Whether the goals they'd set would get them there.

Never one to miss a teachable moment, Jesus responded with a story that warns of the danger of unspecific goals, especially in spiritual things. There's nothing wrong with pie in the sky thinking (especially if there really is pie in the sky), but Jesus wants this man, his disciples and everyone else to check whether they really have got the heavenly goal in sight or not.

How to tell?

Total commitment

Well, is it something they're *totally committed* to? The message to the man on the couch who thinks heaven's assured for him is that *a comfort zone is a very dangerous place to be*. Despite their confident assurance (and did you ever meet anyone who really didn't think their place in heaven was a certainty?) Jesus told a parable which demonstrated that the litmus test for eternity is to ask what their hearts were set on today.

In those days in the Middle East, whenever someone was going to throw a great banquet at some point in the future, they would give those they were inviting a preliminary, "put this in your diary" invitation, with an RSVP. And it seems all those invited said, "I'll be there!"

Subsequently when the actual day of the party arrived, the host would send out messengers to say, "It's all laid out and ready to go, come now."

In the Old Testament we see Queen Esther following that formula when inviting the king and even her enemy Haman to dine with her. In the Jewish culture, without this two-part invitation people would usually not feel really invited – and so were unlikely to actually attend.

Hospitality was massive in that culture. To refuse the second invitation – having responded that you were committed to coming – was not just a breach of social nicety; it could be construed as an act of war!

These invited people said no! (The crowd would gasp as Jesus got to that party of the story.) When these people had been invited twice but knocked it back, and at the last minute too, you would think there had to be some dire emergency to keep them from coming. Let's examine what Jesus said their typical excuses for not following on that commitment were.

> *"One guest after another started making excuses. The first one said, 'I bought some land, and I've got to look it over. Please excuse me.' Another guest said, 'I bought five teams of oxen, and I need to try them out. Please excuse me.' Still another guest said, 'I have just gotten married, and I can't be there.' "* [7]

Possessions, pre-occupation, people

Those were the three excuses. But who goes and buys a field and then goes to look at it *after* the sale? Is it going to have changed since the sale? I've seen a lot of fields and trust me, they don't change that quickly. So what's the point? Why's he going at night anyway? I'm thinking, who buys five yoke of oxen and then afterwards decides it's really important to examine them right away? If any of them had only three legs, he should have spotted that before he paid his money. Couldn't it keep?

And why can't the guy who just got married bring his lovely new wife with him – surely she's not that bad?

The fact is they are all just *excuses*. The Greek word used here means, "to shun or reject". They're a smokescreen. There isn't a single genuine reason for spurning the invitation at all. They just can't be bothered! They said they were coming to the feast, but they weren't committed enough to actually be there! Their goals were too low, aimed all at this world. However we dress it up, God knows our excuses for not making or following through on commitments.

What's keeping you back from fully entering into the life in the Kingdom of God? What's stopping you from setting goals so that you grow and mature in generosity, in spiritual maturity, in Bible knowledge, in commitment to Jesus?

What's holding you back?

What's been holding you back from more fully discovering the purpose God put you on earth for or from developing your spiritual side?

- *Friends?*
- *A job?*
- *Money?*
- *A car?*

- *A hobby?*
- *A habit?*
- *Your past?*
- *Prestige?*
- *What people might say?*

When I was a police officer, I was astounded time and again by people's ability to self-deceive. People I'd arrested and caught red-handed – we called it "bang to rights" – would come to court. As they stood in the dock, you could tell by the look on their face and the words that they said, as the months had passed since they were caught, they had by now convinced themselves that they were totally innocent. They really believed they hadn't committed the crime!

One man I arrested for being drunk and disorderly slurred, "I'm just an innocent stybander!"

I know my heart too, and I know it's possible for us to become masters of self-deception, isn't it? We can convince ourselves, even truly believe some of the time, that our lives, goals and priorities are noble and correct. We can believe that we are okay with God, and he with us, so one day we'll get to share that heavenly kingdom, however we live this life.

Maybe we've accepted the first invitation. We've nodded heavenwards and said as a child or at some point, "Yes please God, heaven sounds good to me, I'll say a few words in prayer if that means I've accepted the invitation."

But the truth hurts when we check ourselves and discover we're actually not correctly focused as we thought. Our goals are just that. Ours. If anything we've asked God to bless our plans, rather than ask him to show us his so we can obey. It gives me no pleasure at all, in fact it chills me to remember that Jesus said *many* will come to him on Judgment Day and find the goals they've set (or failed to make) have left them well short of reaching heaven.

Many people, a lot, a whole bunch, a multitude, will say something like, "Hey Lord, we thought we were on your side! We put some money on the plate, we mumbled through with the choir, we were not bad people, we sometimes even said the prayers!"

And Jesus will say, "I never knew you."

Possessions, pre-occupations and people can hold us back. Don't let it happen. Many people, whether they call themselves believers or not, will choose to keep on walking the easy path of sin, slothfulness and self-deception. Their hope is that in the end it'll line up with the road to salvation, but the road of true commitment to God's kingdom is tough.

Pliable's progress?

As soon as Christian sets out on the road to the Celestial City, he's joined by a companion. The guy is called Pliable (if only people had names that betrayed their character when we first met them, wouldn't life be much easier?). This man Pliable is thrilled to hear of the joys of heaven described in Christian's Bible. He wants those glorious and comforting things read to him. He likes all the good bits.

Pliable wants to know about fanfares, feasts and fun everlasting in heaven, after living however he wants to here on earth. He wants to get to the place where there are no tears, where all is peace and the streets are paved with gold. He tells Christian to hurry because he can't wait to get there!

They've only got a little way along the path when they fall into the cloying mud of the Slough of Despond. Now it's hard going here. Their clothes get filthy. It smells like the inside of a wrestler's laundry basket. He can't see where he's going very well. Getting angry with Christian he shouts at him, *"Is this the happiness you told me of? If we have such ill speed at our first setting out, what may we expect betwixt this and our journey's end?"*

Pliable heaves himself out at the end closest to his own house and goes sulkily back; back to the "cozy" comforts of the good old City of Destruction.

Let me tell you a secret. Any time you want, you can check whether your goals are going in the right direction ultimately. As you are sitting there now, you really can find whether the journey you're making through life is headed toward the Celestial City or not.

Put the book down in a moment if you're brave. Wherever you are and however this book got into your hands you can close your eyes and pray. (Nobody will know except you and God. People might just think you've got a headache or something if they're watching, don't worry about it. Maybe you're not ready for that yet, okay – I understand. I hope you'll keep reading the book.)

Ask God, give God permission to put a spotlight in to search your heart right now, so you can see like he already does: ask the God you can call Father...

- *"Do my goals line up with your direction?"*
- *"Are my priorities right? Do they line up with yours?"*

Count the cost, the cost of saying "yes", and the cost of "no". Who has most wisdom to direct your life? You or God? Maybe in many areas you've been calling all the shots so far. How's that been going – where has it got you, really? Stephen Covey once said, "Be sure that, as you scramble up the ladder of success, it is leaning against the right building."

What would it mean to you to begin to more closely align your life with heaven's direction for you? If you haven't counted the cost, you will have to some day soon because I guarantee you'll encounter some hard going on the way. When the muck hits the fan, some people just bail out. Whatever their name, they are Pliable. They are great at talking about the glory, but they don't want to know when it's gory!

Stacey Padrick wrote about his first Chinese banquet when living in Asia,

> "We assumed they held back in traditional fashion so we could enjoy more. Yet over the course of the next two hours, the dishes kept coming. Well into the banquet, a waiter brought a huge platter of the most glistening and ornately decorated chicken I'd ever seen. Our host excitedly exclaimed, 'This the gold medal!' as he loaded our bowls with succulent meat. But by the time the prized dish had come, Desiree and I could hardly open our mouths for another bite. Only then did we realize the first rounds of dishes were merely appetizers." [8]

Living in a relatively prosperous part of the world I meet people all the time, stuffing themselves on life's appetisers and saving no room for the true meal. Appetisers are good, appetisers are tasty, but appetisers were never intended to satiate our appetite. Their purpose is to stimulate our appetite for the main course.

Make sure when you think about and plot your goals for life you don't just fill it with temporary and earth-bound matters. You could have all kinds of such desires fulfilled, but like even the best appetisers, they'll only partially satisfy. Don't mistake them for what God has prepared to nourish your soul.

You have been invited to a heavenly banquet, so God says,

> *"Why spend money on what is not bread,*
>   *and your labour on what does not satisfy?*
> *Listen, listen to me, and eat what is good,*
>   *and your soul will delight in the richest of fare."* [9]

All the choices you make this week, and the goals we set (or don't set) will betray where your truest allegiance lies. What will you fill your plate with? Our commitment to living God's way can be defined like this: *Doing what God defines best for me, whatever it costs me.*

Unpalatable truths

Pliable didn't stand much of a chance. He'd only heard the promises of everlasting glory. That was the bit of gospel he received. No wonder he embraced it! Sometimes in an effort to be more palatable, Christianity has been falsely portrayed as building a little religious conservatory tagged on the back of the house of your life. All gain, no pain!

Early on in this book I want to warn you; if we're going to be able to press through the dark, smelly muddy bits of life – if you want to come out on the side facing toward heaven, clean off and carry on down the path. We have to know and count the cost of that commitment, the sooner the better.

Ecclesiastes 11:4 (NKJV) says,

> *"He who observes the wind will not sow,*
> *And he who regards the clouds will not reap."*

Another translation renders that, "If you wait for perfect conditions, you'll never get anything done!" [10]

It would be great if we could set goals for a perfect and ideal life and follow them easily. It would be wonderful to be guaranteed of achieving them all, as some of the self-help gurus tell us we can. *If only* the path to heaven was paved with good intentions, but actually in that way lies disaster.

Most people at that Pharisees' party would have had the Torah memorised. The first five books of the Old Testament were taught before any reasonably able child was knee high to a camel. The excuses the people in the story gave might challenge our twenty-first century materialism, but for the first hearers there would no doubt have been a deeper first resonance.

Commitments need courage

The three excuses reflect a passage in Deuteronomy 20 (CEV) giving instructions for war. Before any battle a priest was instructed to go through the ranks with three reasons people could give for not going into battle. Cowardice keeps people from setting and achieving their goals. Because anything worthwhile is only achieved on the other side of a battle of some kind, commitments need courage. So the priest would say,

- *"If any of you have built a new **house**, but haven't yet moved in, you may go home . . . "* (verse 5).
- *"If any of you have planted a **vineyard** but haven't had your first grape harvest, you may go home . . . "* (verse 6).
- *"If any of you are engaged to be **married**, you may go back home and get married . . . "* (verse 7).

Possessions, pre-occupations and *people*. These are the three things that hold the many back from fully entering the kingdom of heaven.

Verse 8 tells us a little more of the root cause behind God's instructions. He knew about their mortgage, he knew about their hobbies, he knew about their family position. God knew all that already. But he knew something more compelling that would keep them back even if they did join the army. That's why this verse told the commanders of the army,

> *"If any of you are **afraid**, you may go home. We don't want you to discourage the other soldiers."*

We sat together as a family recently and watched a documentary about the eruption of Vesuvius which destroyed Pompeii on 23 August AD 79. There was no escaping the terror for the 20,000 inhabitants. Their bodies were petrified in position, buried in 3 metres of wet ashes and cinders. They were found doing whatever they were doing as the end came. It testified clearly what was important to them:

- Some people were locked in the embracing arms of a loved one.

- Many were in the brothel, where the wall paintings are preserved beautifully.
- Others had their hands full of looted gold.

One thing stands out for me as a picture of what commitment really looks like. A Roman centurion stood at the city gate, with his hands still grasping his weapon. He was doing what he had last been told to do by his captain. He didn't know what was happening, at that time even the greatest scholars of the empire knew nothing about volcanoes. But while the earth shook beneath him, as the sky went black and there was no sun, while the pyroplastic flow of ashes and cinders overwhelmed him, he stood firm and faced the inferno. He remained at his post; and was found there hundreds of years later.

God doesn't promise to make following his way easy. He has promised us life in all fullness – the best possible life – when we sign up to be his disciples, but not the *easiest* possible life. We have to push on through even when things get tough. Jesus didn't come to make life easy or safe for us. He knew that playing it safe has its own dangers too.

Two reasons to stay at your post

Your post could be a marriage, a job, a spiritual commitment to pray, or any number of things. Let's look at two reasons to stay the course, two reasons why Moses' army should have resisted the temptation to back off and pack in when the going was about to get tough. Maybe they'll help you stand too.

The first comes from the beginning of that chapter in Deuteronomy, it sets the scene for the announcement to be made allowing the uncommitted to go home.

> *"When you go out to fight against your enemies and you see chariots and horses and an army that outnumbers yours, do not be afraid of them. The LORD your God, who rescued you from Egypt, **will be with you.**"*
>
> (Deuteronomy 20:1, GNB; emphasis added)

I remember as boy walking through a playground area on the council estate I was brought up on, where just days before I'd been beaten up by some kids. But now I had no fear – bring them on! Why? Because this time my Dad was by my side. We shouldn't run when things get tough. The Lord who is a rescuer, the God we get to call Father, has promised his presence with us. If God is for us, who can be against us?

The second reason for us to push through the quitting points to make and fulfil our commitments comes once the priest has made his announcement, and the uncommitted have left the field.

> *"When the officers have finished speaking to the army, **leaders** are to be chosen for each unit."* [11]

God only chooses his best from the ranks of the committed. If you want to lead the band, you have to face the music. Only commitment will get you there.

Commitment gets you there

A few days ago I ran 19 miles in pouring rain and driving wind as part of my training to run the London Marathon this year for charity again.

I have a plan to accomplish that goal. It's clear, specific, measurable, challenging but attainable, and I've written it down and stuck it on the wall. I didn't run because I felt like it. If I waited for good feelings and rosy glows before I set off, I don't think I'd ever set off! But I have a goal in sight, and I'm committed to it. I look forward to the thrill of crossing that line.

There are times on life's journey when you want to give in for sure. Commitments push you through the quitting points and get you to the place where character is built. In a marriage, in relationships with God and people and in leadership, commitments keep you going on the right road, and commitments will keep you there – however tough it gets.

Running the right way

In 1993 a man called Mike Delcavo joined 128 runners in the NCAA Cross-Country championship in Riverside, California. Three miles in he was halfway back in the pack. At a certain point the lead runner made a wrong turn and almost all the others followed him. Mike saw the error, called and motioned to the other runners that they were going the wrong way.

Only five of the 128 runners followed him. The wrong way cut three quarters of a mile off the race, so when the two groups reunited, most of the runners were now in front of Mike. Mike finished first among those that ran the right, more difficult, course but one hundred and third overall. Incredibly, because of protests, the race officials declared the short route the official course. Mike finished one hundred and third even though he ran the right way. He received a name, "Right way Delcavo!"

I know there have been times when you've looked at the

world and noticed that it is not going the right way. Which way are you going? If you go the wrong way, before long you won't be able to tell which is the right way. The world won't reward you for going the right way. I'm talking about character, integrity, how you relate to your family. In fact the world will ridicule you for making the decisions, having the desire and discipline to go the right way, because the right way is usually a lot tougher, but you'll receive a name for going the right way. However many goals I've made or will write down in the future I make this my highest goal; to receive this name. It's the most precious title Jesus bestows on any of his people. In the book of Revelation you can read his promise to award this name. It doesn't necessarily come to the cleverest or most gifted. It comes to those who refocus on inner growth and are not afraid to make and keep commitments.

Follow God's way, press on through, don't shrink back, have the right goal in sight.

Jesus calls you, "Overcomer".

Ponder

- What's stopping you from following God's way for your life? What would it really take to convince you to follow his way?
- Have you been aware of times when it has been tough going, but you were given strength to push through the quitting points?
- Which of the three big snares – *possessions*, *pre-occupation* or *people*, most often has hindered you from stepping out fully toward the Celestial City?

I Don't Have to Worry
if Someone Rejects Me

"Fear knocked at the door.
Faith answered.
No one was there."

In 1993 FBI agents conducted a raid of Southwood psychiatric hospital San Diego, under investigation for medical insurance fraud. After hours of reviewing medical records, the agents were hungry. The agent in charge of the investigation called a nearby pizza parlour to order a quick dinner for his colleagues.

According to www.snopes.com, a site dedicated to exposing urban myths, this isn't one! The following telephone conversation actually took place:

Agent: Hello. I would like to order 19 large pizzas and 67 cans of coke.

Pizza Man: And where would you like them delivered?

Agent: We're over at the psychiatric hospital.

Pizza Man: The psychiatric hospital?

Agent: That's right. I'm an FBI agent.

Pizza Man: You're an FBI agent?

Agent: That's correct. Just about everybody here is.

Pizza Man: And you're at the psychiatric hospital?

Agent: That's correct. And make sure you don't go through the front doors. We have them locked. You will have to go around to the back to the service entrance to deliver the pizzas.

Pizza Man: And you say you're *all* FBI agents?

Agent: That's right. How soon can you have them here?

Pizza Man: And everyone at the psychiatric hospital is an FBI agent?

Agent: That's right. We've been here all day and we're starving.

Pizza Man: How are you going to pay for all of this?

Agent: I have my check book right here.

Pizza Man: And you're all FBI agents?

Agent: That's right. Everyone here is an FBI agent. Can you remember to bring the pizzas and cans to the service entrance at the back? We have the front doors locked.

Pizza Man: I don't think so.

** Click **

Rejection hurts!

Science magazine[12] reported an experiment where they rigged thirteen volunteers up to an MRI machine and measured their brain patterns through the machine when they experienced some kind of rejection. A social rejection showed up in just the same way as a punch! It registered the same way on the scan. One of the scientists who conducted the study wrote, "In the English language we use physical metaphors to describe social pain like 'broken heart' and 'hurt feelings', now we see that there is good reason for this."

A second study suggested rejection may lead to aggressive behaviour, even violence. "Children who might not have been aggressive otherwise will often become aggressive after they have been rejected by their peers. Almost all school shooting incidents, including Columbine, involved rejection by peers," said researcher Dr Jean M. Twenge of San Diego State University.[13]

In one of a series of experiments, students were asked to choose the two people they would want to work with on an individual basis. Half of the students were then told that no one wanted to work with them. The rest were told everyone wanted to work with them. The researchers then had the students play a computer game in which the winner was able to blast the loser with a very loud and unpleasant noise.

The rejected students exhibited more aggression than their peers, tending to blast noise of a higher intensity and for a longer duration, even when they were told it would not be directed towards the individuals who rejected them from the group assignment. "Innocent bystanders are likely to be targets of the aggression of rejected people ..." said Dr Twenge.

Hurt people hurt people

Even without the studies, whether it's not being picked for the team, being snubbed at a party or overlooked for a promotion we thought was due to us, we all know the pain of rejection. We know the dull heartache of being rejected can lead us to wanting to get our own back and that we'll hit out in any direction. We know rejection unresolved can fester and form a crust around a hardened heart, a heart that wants to hurt back. We know hurt people hurt people.

As we go through life, we will be rejected. Sometimes it will be fair, based on the rules of life that say I'm unlikely to get called up to play football for the England squad. Another time you'll be doing your best to co-operate with others and do what you think God wants you to do. Suddenly you'll come up against a brick wall. Someone will malign your motives, doubt your decisions and stamp on your sincerity.

Your heart will cry out for revenge against this person who doesn't respect you. You'll be angry because she didn't smile when you walked by. Even if you couldn't go, you feel stung by the bitter disappointment that you received no invitation. You press it down and live with it as though it didn't really bother you. But it did. You were rejected, and rejection hurts.

Jesus knew about rejection

The apostle John says of Christ, *"He was in the world, and though the world was made through him, the world did not recognise him"*.[14] Even when Jesus identified who he was and what he had come to do – the Son of God come to save us, the Master come to show us the best possible life – the response was not a glad and grateful recognition, but rather the ultimate rejection, his crucifixion.

It seems that early on in his life Jesus had come to terms with the inevitability of rejection. No matter what he did, some people would reject him. He faced that, and kept on walking. He summed up his mission statement, his plan, as follows:

> *"The Son of Man will be betrayed to the chief priests and to the scribes; and they will condemn Him to death and deliver Him to the Gentiles; and they will mock Him, and scourge Him, and spit on Him, and kill Him. And the third day He will rise again."* [15]

We too have to face a brutal fact. We will be rejected. Not because like some people we just love to nurse our hurts and bleat forever about our rejection. Not because we have a persecution complex. Not because we are paranoid (though even if you are it doesn't mean they're not all out to get you). We know we'll be rejected, because Jesus warned his followers straight:

> *"If the world hates you, you know that it hated Me before it hated you. If you were of the world, the world would love its own. Yet because you are not of the world, but I chose you out of the world, therefore the world hates you. Remember the word that I said to you, 'A servant is not greater than his master.' If they persecuted Me, they will also persecute you. If they kept My word, they will keep yours also."* [16]

This was brought home most forcefully to me as I watched Mel Gibson's film, *The Passion of the Christ*, this passage coming as it did as a flashback amid the sufferings of Christ.

I took it as a prophecy for the days ahead for the church. However you act, whatever you do, some people *will* ridicule, reject and revile you. A student is not above his master, if it happened to Jesus, it'll happen to his followers. We have to face this fact, follow him through the path of rejection, and not be put off by it.

The Bible tells us,

> *"If it is possible, as far as it depends on you, live at peace with everyone."* [17]

But how?

How do I handle personal relationships in a world where people will reject me? How do I live and conduct my relationships such that, as far as it depends on me, I can live at peace with others? Let me give you five "A"s to help describe your part. Then their part is up to them.

1. Assume the best

Many years ago a traveller approached an old man sitting at the city gate of Rome, and asked what the people of the city were like. The old man asked the traveller where he had come from and he told him that he had come from Rimini. "What were the people like in Rimini?" The old man asked.

"Those people were rude, stingy, overbearing and horrible. They treated me terribly and I couldn't stand to be among them."

"You will find the people here are just the same," said the old man.

A few hours later another traveller from Rimini appeared at

the city gate and asked the same question, "What are the people here in Rome like?"

"What were the people like in Rimini?"

"They were polite, friendly, generous charming and great company."

"You will find people here are just the same."

If you expect to be rejected, chances are you will be. If you think people will ignore you at the party, you'll stand in a corner with a face like a bag of spanners and people won't come and talk to you. I've had someone come up to me with a terribly angry face at the end of a service who said they were a visitor. They'd gone off to the back of the church and glowered at people and surprisingly no-one came to talk to them. "This is such an unfriendly church!"

In my experience people rise or fall to your level of expectations. If you believe in people and expect them to respond well to you, they will go the extra mile trying to prove you right.

One study showed that 90% of prison inmates said at least one of their parents had repeatedly said, "You'll end up in jail someday." Expectations placed on people are powerful! Victor Frankl said, "If we take people as they are, we make them worse. If we take them as they should be, we help them become what they can be."

God believes in you! So if you've never been one to trust people and put your faith in them, change your way of thinking and begin believing in others! Your life will quickly improve. If you believe and expect the best in others, you mark yourself out from the crowd immediately, and people will be drawn to you because of that different attitude you have, because most people only hear negatives about themselves.

Jesus sent his disciples out on mission with a strategy based on assuming the best about others:

> *"When you come to a town or village, go in and look for someone who is willing to welcome you, and stay with him until you leave that place. When you go into a house, say, 'Peace be with you.'"* [18]

It's *only* if people withdraw from us that we need go around shaking any dust off our feet.

Sometimes articles I read or people I talk with about sharing our faith with others make it sound as if everyone's against us.

In my experience that's just not so. In today's society, most people feel isolated. Any strong sense of community has become rare and is valuable. People are looking for love, looking for community, and looking for God. I believe there are all kinds of people who are really keen and open to believe in God; people who pray regularly, who love their families and want them to know the blessing and favour of God. Jesus called such people, "People of peace". We can connect such people to the God who's looking for them.

Some people bemoan a world that's hostile at worst and indifferent at best to the good news about Jesus. But as I go through life I'm always bumping into people of peace! I find all kinds of people who are open, friendly and willing to chat. Many are open to a word of prayer offered sincerely too. In fact, as I've shared and listened to people, I don't think I've ever had anyone refuse an offer I've made to pray with them. So, are you generally a person who believes the best? That's a Jesus-like attitude.

2. Agree with others

In Matthew 5:25 Jesus said, *"Agree with your adversary quickly"* (NKJV). When you tell someone he or she is wrong, even if you are attacking a position, you can be perceived as attacking them (their intelligence or knowledge). Their guard goes up. They become like a hedgehog. It's an obvious fact of human nature that we all hate to be wrong, and we never hate it more than when it's becoming increasingly obvious! Self-esteem is easily bruised and wounded, especially when you are dealing with a person in whom it is already fragile.

Be agreeable. Even if in your opinion the other person is 100% wrong, take a moment and a deep breath and ask, "Is this really important?" If not, why disagree over it?

Being agreeable means you are just the kind of person who agrees with other people. It's about being easy going, recognising that there are all kinds of things that really are not worth arguing over.

If you become an agreeable person as you travel through life, you'll create less friction and go faster and further, because you'll meet with less resistance. Other people will be glad to help you and will want to get along with you. When people like you, they are far more willing to co-operate with you because they trust you. Assume the best about people, and be agreeable.

3. Accept others

We are hardwired to seek the acceptance of others. A baby will spend ages looking into Mum's face, to see if he or she is accepted and loved. As we grow up we look to the face of others around us to see whether they think we are valuable, cherished, respected, wanted, important etc. Whether we admit it or not, everyone has a deep need to be accepted by other people, even people we don't know.

Think about a meeting between two people. All kinds of things in this other person's face and body language will either embrace us or reject us. With the people you talk to today, be aware that they will be searching for acceptance as they look into your eyes. Looking for a smile, looking to be accepted so that they can be happy and relax in your presence.

My grandmother used to have a plaque on the wall that declared, "It only takes thirteen muscles to smile and a hundred and twelve muscles to frown, so why waste energy?"

A Chinese proverb says, "A man without a smiling face must not open a shop." We all know relationships are so important in every walk of life, don't we? I have found an amazing thing: the more I smile, the more I smile. And if I smile at people, they smile back! The starting point of *being* liked is to like other people. Do unto others as you'd have them do unto you. Express that with a smile.

If you not only refuse to belittle others but actively choose instead to accept and even celebrate them, if you regularly and sincerely express deeply felt and unconditional acceptance, you will find that the other person's self-esteem and self-image are significantly affected. You are far less likely to have a hard time with them!

4. Appreciate others

Thanking someone has enormous power. The simplest way to show appreciation is to just come out and say it. I've heard it said that the two greatest jobs of a leader are to set direction and to say thank you.

I find that if you say thank you for small things, people will be happy to help you do bigger things. Saying "thank you" can become a good habit. Saying thank you to your spouse, thank you to your kids, saying, "thank you" to someone who serves you or helps you, someone who makes time to see you. Thank them for their time. Thank them for their comments, thank them for their kindness. Thank people for just about everything you can think of.

Write some thank-you notes this week and send them to people! Thank-you notes and cards are great for building relationships and raising someone's self-esteem. Something that takes a few minutes for you to write can be remembered for months – what a great investment! The more thankful you are, the more you'll have cause to be thankful.

Whenever the apostle Paul wrote to churches, he seemed to be looking for ways to catch them doing something right so he could thank them and commend them. Sometimes he did that to a church corporately, but often he'd run together a list of names and show appreciation for individuals. He didn't just press "Reply to all!" Paul wanted to take the opportunity to individually notice and commend someone and express gratitude and appreciation.

A great way to show appreciation is to genuinely praise someone. Haven't you ever noticed the way a child who's been feeling down will suddenly straighten up their back, smile and get back enthusiastically to the task at hand when they hear genuine praise from someone who they respect? Nothing has greater power to boost flagging spirits than an appropriate expression of praise and approval. How do you praise?

- Praise *swiftly*. Do it as soon as possible, don't put it off. The sooner you praise, the more powerful it is. Some organisations wait a whole year for appraisal time before someone hears a "well done". That's pretty useless. Give a gold watch early.
- Praise *specifically*. Tell people what it is and why it is they are receiving your gratitude, admiration and praise.
- Praise *publicly*. If you really have to correct a person, try whenever possible to do it in private. But praise in front of others. People will say they hate this, but in my experience they don't really! In fact the more you praise someone, the greater the boost for the person.

5. Attend to others

We all hate to be ignored, whether by a waiter, a wife or a workmate. Life is all about attention. You pay attention to that which is important to you. Wherever your attention goes, you go too. In relationships, everyone has radar about whether you are paying them attention or not. And attached to that is an invisible gauge indicating to them how important you think they are. You give your attention to people and things you value most. It's been said the opposite of love is not hate, but indifference. Apathy is awful.

If you don't appreciate people or things, you'll ignore them. They'll see you as rejecting them. As we saw earlier, rejected people easily become embittered, angry and defensive. The people who are most effective in human relationships are those who are best at paying attention to others. That's about *listening*.

If you followed me around closely you'd soon see that this is an area that I need to work on! Especially when you have the situation where you bump into someone out shopping or in a parking lot and ask them, "How are you?" Then they have the audacity to actually start to tell you!

You can hear without listening. Really listening to others is hard work! But listening is the measure of attention. Listening is how you demonstrate acceptance and value to another person. If you listen well to others, you are telling them, "You are valuable. You are important."

One of the most common causes of friction and disunity is that we don't really listen to each other. Better listening means fewer mistakes, greater wisdom, more friends, less aggro, and much more trust.

Whenever someone listens to us, we trust that person more. The fastest way for two people to build trust is that they listen appreciatively and attentively to each other, without interrupting or presuming you know what the other person is going to say – because you never learn anything while you're speaking. Emerson wrote, "Every man I meet is in some way my superior, and I can learn of him."

The average person speaks at about 150 words per minute, while with concentration you can listen at about 600 words per minute. The gap can create tension and cause the listener to lose focus. Often high energy people like me will try to fill the gap by finding other things to do, like nodding and smiling and daydreaming, all the time thinking about their next project. Like when we drive a car, how many times have you got where you wanted to be on auto pilot? I want to learn to direct that excess energy positively by concentrating on the person I'm talking with. I think it can build great patience and self-discipline in us as we listen, as well as self-esteem in the person we're listening to, if we can just stay focused on the person and not be distracted, or jump in with our response.

Dale Carnegie advised, "You can make more friends in two weeks by becoming a good listener than you can in two years trying to get other people interested in you." [19]

Listen with your eyes. Listen as you would like to be listened to. Listen for what they are saying and what they are not saying. Face the speaker directly. Lean forward slightly, toward them. Watch their eyes and mouth closely. This all silently says to the other person, "I am paying complete attention to you." Great learners are great listeners – who become great leaders.

But you'll still get rejected . . .

You try to live at peace with everyone, as far as it depends on you. You do that by assuming the best about them, being agreeable, accepting, appreciating and paying attention to them. Someone who will consistently live like that will find all kinds of open doors in life. People of peace will open their homes and their hearts to you. You will make all kinds of friends in unexpected ways and places. You will enjoy the favour of God and people. But still, some will reject you.

What then? Jesus went on to tell his disciples what to do when they got the cold shoulder of condemnation or even the five fingered fist of fellowship!

> *"If someone won't welcome you or listen to your message, leave their home or town. And shake the dust from your feet at them."* [20]

That's a sign which says, "I will have nothing more to do with you." Jesus had given his disciples the authority to speak for him and to do miracles on his behalf. You'd think everyone would welcome that. But Jesus was preparing them for inevitable rejection by some.

I've outlined what I believe to be the right way forward in relationships. However there can come a point when you can reject those who reject you. It's a way down the line, but there will always be people who will trample your pearls under their porky little feet if you'll let them. Remember those words of warning from Jesus. You have to be careful who you open up to and really trust, you might live to regret it.

It's not usually the openly hostile you have to worry about. Jesus warned his friends about people who'll smile at you to your face while stabbing you in the back. It's the flattering, friendly looking wolves in sheepskin coats that cause the most damage. There are some people who will rock the boat then moan to everyone that you have led them into stormy seas!

I hope I've made it clear how we're to go the extra mile in relationships. When someone opposes you, Jesus says the general rule is don't argue, just move on. *Move on* to the next person or place God leads you. If you argue with a fool, anyone walking past might not be able to tell who's who. If you fight with a skunk, it's hard to come out smelling of roses!

Don't waste your time with people whose minds are already made up, I prefer to spend time with people who are hungry to find out the truth about God.

Paul wrote to the Galatians,

> *"Am I now trying to win the approval of men, or of God? Or am I trying to please men? If I were still trying to please men, I would not be a servant of Christ."* [21]

I'll be looking at that next. Sometimes there's a choice to make. Who are you going to live to please? People in this temporary life, or your heavenly Father for eternity?

When I was in the police I worked with a senior officer who was a God-hater. Because he hated God, he made life miserable for me. He did whatever he could to try to make me look bad, or incompetent, or prim and proper or a hypocrite. He made it clear that he was the boss and the only way to succeed in this department was to allow this treatment to go unchallenged. I prayed. I put up with it. Until I challenged him, face to face.

I confronted him about his attitude. One day after he'd just had another go at me, I waited until there were just the two of us in the office. Then I said, "I believe that I am a man chosen by God to accomplish great things. I have a destiny. The God I love loves me. He has promised to bless me. This same God has said that because I am a blessed man, whoever blesses me will be blessed and whoever curses me will be cursed." That got his attention. "With the greatest respect, you'd better stop harassing me, because you don't want my God on your case."

I had no further trouble from that man. In fact within a week he had left the department.

There will be times when you'll be doing your best following Jesus and some people won't like the way you're going or what you're doing. At times like that, we have to be strong.

We don't look for these times, but *never* let someone stamp on your dreams. Never let them tell you "God can't." when you know he can. Never let them tell you, "God won't," when he's told you he will!

I confront that! I stand against small visions and weak hearts. I was saved for a great purpose and God will do amazing things in my life. I will not have someone else's negativity or unbelief drag me down or hold me back. And I don't have to worry about people rejecting me. I'm an "attack" sheep of the good shepherd!

Jesus said, "You're going out into the middle of a world full of wolves, and you're sheep." That's a scary picture isn't it? So, he says,

> "Make sure you little sheep act like snakes. Be on the look out. Be shrewd. Be wise. Be discreet. Be careful. Don't be like a fox who wants to trick others, but make sure you're like a snake. A snake knows when to keep quiet, a snake knows a little self-defence and can get to a place of safety quickly. At the same time, you sheep be harmless as doves. Fly away wounded rather than fight if you can, because you're made for love not war." [22]

If some people reject me, Jesus said they're not really rejecting me, they are rejecting him. And he will never reject me.

Exercise

- Go through the five 'A's again. Rate yourself 1 to 10 on each. Which one do you need to do most work on to improve your relationships? Which one do you score highest on?
- Better still, get someone who knows you well to rate you.
- Men, if you're really brave – ask your wife . . .

I Don't Have to Please Everyone

"To his dog, every man is Napoleon;
hence the constant popularity of dogs."
(Aldous Huxley)

A little background

In the Bible and in Jewish writings throughout history to the present day, the Amalekites represent the archetypal enemy of the Jews. Modern Judaism refers to Amalek as "the eternal foe", and metaphorically equates the evil of the Nazis and anyone else who has tried to eradicate them with Amalekites.

Anyone who starts to look through the Bible in general and the Old Testament in particular will at times encounter hard passages where nations are attacked and it seems that God not only sanctions but in fact commands the action! What kind of loving God would do that?

Before coming to the principle I want to draw out from an incident in the life of a character called King Saul, I need to try to clear up a hard issue right at the start without which some of you will be distracted. Here's the question; "What's all this about God killing Amalekites?"

This week my newspaper details continual unrest in the Middle East and an act by Israel of killing the "spiritual leader of the militant group Hamas", I put the paper down and open my Bible, only to find an account of the God we Christians serve ordering Israel to totally wipe out a group of people. What's going on there? Isn't it proof of a spiteful, nasty God in the Old Testament?

Looking at history helps explain it. The Amalekites were a fierce nomadic tribe of people who routinely and consistently attacked and tried to kill the children of Israel. They tried it first in the desert of Sinai just after the escape from Egypt – the Bible says that in order to demonstrate that they did not fear or respect the God of the Israelites, in that weakened condition Amalek immediately attacked "the weak and helpless" of the Israelites.

Soon thereafter and totally without provocation, Amalek made a full frontal attack on Israel, who were nowhere near them and not threatening their land. There was no reason for it – this attack was altogether an act of aggression and attempted genocide. God there and then pronounced judgment on Amalek. He declared that he would oppose them as a nation and destroy them as a national entity – sometime in the future.

You can only test the patience of God so long. The people of Amalek continued the behaviour of their forefathers, oppressing and attacking Israel for a further 400 years! And here's an amazing thing, during those same years the Amalekites were welcomed into Israel as immigrants. There was a period of "amnesty" where God gave the individuals within the nation centuries to reform their ways.

They didn't do it. They harboured their resentment. Nursed their grudges. So it was only after hundreds of years of opportunity and influences to change, during which they continued – and actually escalated – atrocities and violence against Israel, that God decided to impose the judgment he had given centuries earlier. Perhaps that helps put what took place next in context.

Specific instructions

God was very specific in his instructions to Israel's new king, Saul. "Go in and destroy everyone and everything – don't let there be anything left to contaminate or threaten again." Here's how the great Jewish historian Josephus described what happened:

> "Saul preserved their king and governor ... as if he preferred the fine appearance of the enemy to the memory of what God had sent him about. The multitude were also guilty, together with Saul; for they spared the herds and the flocks, and took them for prey, when God had commanded they should not spare them. They also carried off with them the rest of their wealth and riches; but if there

were any thing that was not worthy of regard, that they destroyed." [23]

God gave them victory over their greatest enemies, and it says in 1 Samuel 15:8 that if they saw anything they thought was "worthless or despised", they had no problem getting rid of that – anything no-one wanted anyway. But King Saul kept their king alive. Josephus says it was because he was tall and good looking – make of that what you will.

They made sure they kept the good stuff, cattle, sheep, gold and silver. "All that was good" – good in their eyes that is, because God had already made clear that as far as he was concerned there wasn't *anything* good there. God had his opinion, they had theirs.

The test

God was testing the king and the people. This was to be the supreme assessment of whether this new king was up to the job. Was Saul really the man to lead – to establish them as God's chosen people in the land? It boiled down to one thing. Would he obey what God told him – or just do his own thing. Saul failed miserably.

The Lord sent the prophet Samuel to go and confront Saul, who was in the middle of a victory party in his own honour. Saul came up smiling, "Hi Samuel, I did the job just like God told me."

"Baa ..."

"Really?" says Samuel, "Why do you look a little sheepish?"

"Mooooo ..."

"Okay," said Samuel. "Who's doing the brilliant farmyard impressions? What's that noise?"

It was the sound of disobedience. The sight of someone doing what they thought best. The smell of half-heartedness. It stank to high heaven.

Now Saul of course did what most people would do in that position. What you and I would do. He rationalises his actions, he makes excuses, he shades the truth a little.

He said, "I did it! I went on the mission, just like I was told. I did okay, we trounced them didn't we? I captured the king ... checkmate ... won the battle. I have utterly destroyed the baddies." *But, now wait for it, because here's the kicker:*

"But *the people* ...

... the people" (look at the passage, you'll see they get two mentions), " ... *they* wanted to keep the best stuff. I was thinking maybe we could sacrifice some of it to God?"

Lame excuses didn't impress Samuel and it goes without saying God saw right through them. From that day on, Saul's days as king were numbered. He'd fallen at the first fence. He'd failed at his job, which was just to do what God told him. Instead Saul did what *he* thought best in the circumstances. Why?

> **King Saul did not do what God wanted to do,**
> **because he wanted to keep the people happy.**

Proverbs 29:25 says, *"The fear of man brings a snare"* (NKJV). We know that's true don't we? It'll keep on tripping you up and it will stop you from moving forward.

Contrasting kings

Let's contrast King Saul with the King of kings. How did the Master, Jesus, deal with this pressure you and I face – the pressure to please people? Here's a time when he faced that really powerfully.

> *"He then began explaining things to them: 'It is necessary that the Son of Man proceed to an ordeal of suffering, be tried and found guilty by the elders, high priests, and religion scholars, be killed, and after three days rise up alive.' He said this simply and clearly so they couldn't miss it. But Peter grabbed him in protest. Turning and seeing his disciples wavering, wondering what to believe, Jesus confronted Peter. 'Peter, get out of my way! Satan, get lost! You have no idea how God works.'"* [24]

Follow Jesus' progression through the gospels, and witness a steely determination that kept him walking in obedience toward an appointment with a cross. And he didn't seem to have a problem saying no. Even to large crowds. At one point a whole village full of people with legitimate and real needs. They said, "Stay here with us – and do what we want you to do..."

Jesus said, "Uh uh, gotta go. I only do what I see the Father doing."

His family tried to distract him.

His enemies rose against him.

Now even his closest friends wanted (with the best of intentions) to pull him off track.

How did Jesus resist the pressure to please people – to raise himself above trying to please everyone else – so that he could please his Father? Learn this, and it will help you do the same, which is huge in mastering the art of living the full life.

King Jesus did what God wanted him to do because . . .

1. Jesus was clear about his Mission

Like any good mission statement you can put it in one sentence. It's summed up in that verse we kicked off the book with: *"I came so they can have real and eternal life, more and better life than they ever dreamed of"* (John 10:10, *The Message*). He came to give abundant and eternal life to you and me, better than we could ever imagine. The only way to accomplish that was through his own self-sacrifice. Which leads on to the next reason Jesus did what God wanted him to do.

2. Jesus was clear about the Cost

> *"The nation's leaders, the chief priests, and the teachers of the Law of Moses will make the Son of Man suffer terribly. He will be rejected and killed, but three days later he will rise to life."* [25]

That's what he told his friends. They didn't understand it, they couldn't comprehend it. Peter couldn't stand to hear about the suffering of Jesus. The furore surrounding Mel Gibson's film *The Passion of the Christ* shows us that little has really changed on that score. Watching the film you want the agony to just stop. You have to admit that parts of what Christ went through are so barbaric, so distasteful, we don't even want to contemplate them even if we're separated by thousands of years from them.

And what do you do when you don't like the sound of what God is asking you to do? Usually you try to do something else instead. But not Jesus, because . . .

3. Jesus was clear about the Action *he had to take*

He knew he was God's solution to our greatest problem. He knew his job was to change the situation by changing our destinies. He knew there was only one way. He knew what had to be done. He didn't put it off. He didn't wait for an easier time or a better day. He didn't wait until the problems were all cleared up and sorted out. He took the necessary action!

Oliver Cromwell said, "Do not trust to the cheering, for the same persons would shout as much if you were going to be hanged."

Jesus didn't listen to the crowds who wanted to crown him king on Palm Sunday, because he knew how quickly that fickle tide of popular opinion would turn. He trusted himself to no man for he knew what was in a man. He trusted his Father, and he just kept heading toward the cross. That was his mission. Unlike King Saul, he would carry it out to the letter, along the way fulfilling hundreds of prophecies written centuries beforehand as he did so.

When you're clear about the mission, ready to count the cost of achieving it, and prepared to take the necessary action to do what it takes – you're unstoppable! You are assured of accomplishing what you set out to do, and it won't just be about trying to please other people.

Swayed by the people

King Saul was swayed by the people, distracted away from God's purposes, because he wasn't really clear what his mission was.

What about you? What's your mission?

What on earth are you here on earth for right now?

If you're not clear about that, how will you accomplish it? What is there to prevent you running round through the rest of your life trying to please everyone; in the end pleasing no-one, ultimately missing out on a shed-load of blessings that were yours for the asking, and falling short of fulfilling God's plan for you?

To start to answer that question, let me try to answer another one I've puzzled over myself. Different books give different definitions on this:

> ## What's the difference between having a *mission*, having a *vision*, and having a *goal*?

▶ A ***mission statement*** is a short statement of purpose.
My local church's mission statement reads, *"To extend the kingdom of God ... one life at a time ... by becoming more like Jesus, one day at a time!"* Your mission answers the question, "What have you come to do?" Your organisation's mission statement answers the question, "What specifically won't happen without you?" It should be really short, memorable, and able to be easily understood by a twelve-year-old. Remember Jesus' mission statement? *"I have come that they may have life."*

▶ A ***vision*** is a detailed description of the preferred future.
It is longer than the mission statement and looks forward to an eventual outcome, the promised land, the new future, It answers the question, "What will it look like when we get there?" It's a dream. A good vision comes from having the courage to dream a big dream. It's not always the most talented or best-educated who accomplish the greatest things, rather it's those who refuse

to limit, or put brackets on, their thinking. They reach for the now invisible future knowing you only have power for today when you have vision for tomorrow. Every day I see a note on my wall that says, "Dream no small dreams, for they stir not the hearts of men." [26]

▶ **Goals** are steps to be accomplished on the way to completing the vision.

The goals should be written *after* the mission statement and vision, because goals answer the question, "What do you have to do to get the mission and the vision accomplished?" If you really *want* to write a "To Do" list, maybe another word for a "To Do" list with a direction is "goals"!

What's your purpose?

What's your purpose? Or are you just existing? So many people are.

Henry David Thoreau said, "Most men lead lives of quiet desperation – and go to the grave with the song still in them." Why? Talking to people about this subject often, it saddens me when I find they've fallen into one of the traps that keep people more interested in making a good living than leaving a great legacy:

1. My job *is my purpose*

A study this week reported what men tend to talk about – sport and work. What's the first question between men? "What do you *do*?" A woman may answer, "I'm a doctor." But even though she went into it to help and heal people, now she spends more time dealing with a mountain of paperwork than seeing patients. She's trapped in a lie that sees a job as a purpose. When your job and your purpose in life are aligned – that's perfect! But many people would have to say that isn't their experience.

If your job is your purpose, what happens on the day when you find yourself, "redundant", which according to my dictionary means "no longer necessary, a non-essential". When I was in the police I remember so many people who seemed to live for the day when they took the early retirement at the end of twenty-five years service, then they dropped dead before drawing scarcely any pension. Your purpose *has to* be bigger than your job!

2. My role *is my purpose*

"I'm a wife and mother." Brilliant! That's great. But who will you be when the nest is empty?

In the Old Testament a woman called Naomi defined herself by those roles, but when the roles changed she ended up changing her name to "Marah", which means "bitter".

I meet lots of people who defined themselves by a role, even in church life, and when that went they ended up bitter and twisted. This is all tied in with your view of the kind of god God is. Does he just like you when you perform well? Or does he love who you are?

Thankfully when you go to the end of the story in the last chapter of the book of Ruth, you see that God had a bigger picture, a better dream than she could see by herself right then.

3. I'm not currently *fulfilling my purpose*

Do you know what happens when God gives a procrastinator a great idea? NOTHING! Sometimes we think, "I'll just do life for a while, then when it gets a bit quieter, or I'm less busy, or I've got my PhD, then I'll make sure to make time to discover and do fully what God has planned for me."

The stories of King Arthur's court and the Holy Grail always include the romantic figures Lancelot, Guinevere and Arthur. The stories often centre on the search for the Holy Grail. Percival was not Arthur's cleverest knight. He spent years searching out the Grail.

He went to foreign lands, fought many battles, saved damsels in distress, you know the kind of thing. His companions fell away. Some became mercenaries to fight for money. Others became tenant farmers or merchants. Some died on the road. But Percival continued. Something in his heart wouldn't let him let go of the search for the Holy Grail.

Finally he goes to the castle of a king to ask the whereabouts of the Grail. The king says, "You're my honoured guest – let's have a party first, then we'll talk about that." The night draws on, the candles burn down. Then the king has Percival thrown out. Why?

"Because," the king says, "the grail was placed in front of you three times tonight, and you did not even see it or notice it."

Call off the search! Seize the moment. Make no mistake, you *are* doing a mission. Either God's, or your own, or the one someone else mapped out for you.

You may delay, but time isn't waiting. What will it be, a year or two from now, that you wish you'd started today? Stop making excuses.

What's that in your hand?

Now is the time to discover and get committed to what God wants you to do to make the rest of your life the best of your life.

Moses discovered one day out in the desert that holy ground was right there at his feet. God opened his eyes to that. All those years Moses had been working away, and standing on holy ground. He hadn't even noticed.

As my friend Christine Noble once told me in a message that changed my life, the very thing Moses held in his hand was what God used to do the miracles. *What's that in your hand?* Now is the time to go after your mission!

Ever feel like you're in the wrong place? Let me ask you another question. Name a wrong musical note. There aren't any are there? So how come we have disharmony? Because the beautiful notes aren't in the right place. There's no rhythm to them. There's no rest either (a musical term), so they don't know where they fit in to the song. All you end up with is chaos and noise. If you don't know where you fit in God's song for you, you'll never feel you're in the right place. God wants you to find your place in his purposes!

At the age of twelve Jesus said he knew he had to be about his Father's business. Then Jesus became an artisan. He learned his trade as a builder, working in his earthly father's business. But there was a restlessness inside.

At some point he downed tools, neatly folded his apron, washed the sawdust off his hands, and walked, step by step, into his destiny. Isn't there a call to something greater, a *restlessness* in you too? If we don't suppress it, that will lead us on to the next level.

The fourth thing that keeps people feeling unfulfilled, trapped and outside of God's will is the lie that started my thinking about this book. It's the lie that says . . .

4. My "To Do" list *is my purpose*

You know by now that I don't like "To Do" lists. Maybe *you* do, if so, think about a typical one for a minute. What do they look like? Where would the God-stuff fit in?

- *Ring Fred*
- *Sort out kid's school thing*
- *Go to butchers*
- *Write to complain*
- *Collect flowers*
- *Learn list of Spanish verbs*
- *Pay electricity bill*
- *Worry about the above*
- *Pray*
- *Read the Bible*
- *Worship Jesus*

Prayer, Bible study, worship, serving God by serving others. Aren't these down at the bottom of the list somewhere?

Well here's what I suggest you "To Do list lovers" do with your list: *Flip the list over!* The Bible says, *"the first will be last"* [27] doesn't it?

Or how about, *"Seek ye first the kingdom of God and his righteousness; and all these things shall be added unto you."* [28]

Exercises

Look at the shield of Sir Percival on the next page. Get ready to seize the moment.

In the coat of arms, draw in each of the four quadrants something representative of some of the gifts, talents, attitudes or

[handwritten margin note: It's true we experienced seek first the Kingdom of God & righteousness & all these shall be added unto you]

abilities that God has given you. (You're so full of gifts from God, you might need to rough it out on bigger paper instead.) Spend a little time quietly praying before you do this. Don't pull yourself down or think, "I can't..." With God's help, you can! It's a really useful exercise I have done with my church and people said they felt released to try all kind of new things afterwards.

Have a go at writing your personal *mission* statement? Just a line or two, about what you believe right now God has put you here to do. It doesn't have to be word perfect, but have a go. You could write it in here:

..... *prison ministries* ....
.... *design banners of love for God*

Find the mission God has for you – and you'll find that you really don't have to please everyone!

I Don't Have to Be Fearful over Finances

"Can't buy me love..."
(Lennon & McCartney)

What made him do it?

Judas Iscariot was responsible for one of the most terrible crimes ever committed. It involved a betrayal of trust on a massive scale, leading to the death of an innocent man, the murder of one who trusted him. He was a man thought incredibly gifted by other people, but his character was deeply flawed. What made him do it? His love of money. Money is a commodity that can corrupt people. Many people say that "money is *the* root of all evil". But the Bible does not actually say that. Look again:

*"For the **love** of money is a root of **all kinds** of evil."*

(1 Timothy 6:10, NKJV; emphasis added)

The Bible says money is neither good nor bad, God sees it as a minor thing. Jesus called it a small thing. What you do with the small thing is the big thing.

Think about what's in your pocket or your purse right now. You can't determine where the money in your hands has come from. It could have been in a very rich man's wallet. It could have been someone's last bit of change. It could have been stolen, or funded a crime. You don't know its *history*, but now you have the power and a responsibility to decide its *future*.

Most people would be shocked to discover that Jesus talked more about money than heaven or hell. In fact he said that what you do with your money would be the *acid test* of your faith! So, is it genuine – or counterfeit?

What will you use it for? How much have you wasted so far? Will you spend it on yourself, give it away or put it in a bank?

Faithful administration vs. frantic acquisition

There's no such thing as a self-made man. Everything you have came to you because God gives it. Psalm 24:1 (NIV) says,

"The earth is the LORD's and everything in it."

That means nothing truly belongs to us, it actually belongs to God, and he's watching how we handle it. We think of wages as what we've earned. On the contrary, whenever we receive money and material things, we're not getting what we deserve (otherwise poor beggars in poverty right now are just getting what they deserve aren't they?).

The truth is we should cultivate the attitude of gratitude. We are recipients of the grace of God. According to many passages, including for example the parable of the talents in Matthew 25, we're like managers of a trust fund and will be held to account for what we've been given. There'll be no money in heaven, and the streets are paved with gold. Right now God gives us time, talents and treasure to teach us and test us. The key attitude to it should be faithful administration rather than frantic acquisition. Ultimately God wants you to care more about giving than getting.

God especially uses money to teach us to be generous like him. I read in the paper the other day that the average teenager in the West will easily have a million pounds go through his or her hands before they retire. An awful lot of money comes to many of us, if we added it up across a lifetime – and how many of us when we are eventually called to account by God will shake our heads in disbelief that we squandered an incredible amount?

The problem is the money doesn't pass through our hands does it? Instead it gets stuck in our grubby mitts, or doesn't get passed on the way he'd want it to.

Fear over finances?

Money fears and financial fears rank very highly in our lives.

Just this week a survey revealed that 40% of rows in marriage are over money. Newspaper headlines warn of mounting debts in Britain soaring to over a trillion pounds. Unsustainable levels of credit have so many people in over their heads: worrying about it, hoarding it and keeping it all for themselves.

It does not matter whether we are rich or poor, at times we all worry about money. Media mogul Ted Turner once said, "Bill Gates has got $80 billion, I've only got $8 billion – at times I think I'm a complete failure." At the heart of worry over money is **FEAR**. Someone once said Fear is "False Evidence Appearing Real". Financial fear, as with all fear, tries to stop us from being all that God wants us to be.

Wouldn't it be great to become more generous people, free of concern over money, increasingly giving cheerfully to be used by the God who gave it to you? The good news is there is a way to achieve this – God has an antidote to your financial fear.

God's guarantee

> "God is able to make all grace abound to you, so that in all things at all times, having all that you need, you will abound in every good work." [29]

What a promise! God has put himself on record in the Bible about his ability to do what many of us feel unable to do. He said to those who follow the way of the Master of the full life that he is able to make *all* grace "super-abound" to you so that, at all times, and in *all* things, having *all* that you need, you will overflow and be super-abundant in *every* good work.

Did you notice all the "alls" in that passage? That's God's guarantee and you can take it to the bank. His word is true in every place, time and circumstance, better than any currency or the bond of any government! There's no doubt about it, no cause for concern. This is not like the endowment mortgage I took out in the 1980s that is now unable to meet its promises. It's not like the many pensions that under-perform or don't pay out at all!

However, there is a condition attached. It depends on your *attitude*. Follow some simple principles and I guarantee you will be able to abound in *every* good work.

I know to some people that sounds far too good to be true – like those offers that come through the door every week, but I am convinced of this from what the Bible teaches, and I have proved it time and again in my own experience – even in how this book came into your hands, where God provided in the most amazing way!

The principles to live free of fear in this area of finance really work. Are you ready to see how?

God has a great plan for your *C.A.S.H.*

> ## Cash = Contentment, Ask, Sow, Honesty

Contentment

> *"Godliness with contentment is great gain. For we brought nothing into the world, and we can take nothing out of it."*
>
> (1 Timothy 6:6–7, NIV)

That's true of everyone. When we're born we don't have much and when we die we don't get to keep anything, we leave "everything". There are no pockets in a shroud, nor will you ever see a hearse pulling a trailer.

Do you know why the Bible talks about "learning contentment"? – because it doesn't come naturally. Someone once asked J.D. Rockefeller, "How much will it take to make you happy?" He replied, "Just a little bit more." If you can't learn contentment, you'll never have enough. Not even God will be able to meet all your *wants*, even though he is able to meet your *needs*.

Contentment is about not comparing or trying to keep up with the Joneses. It starts with not complaining, not getting jealous and coveting the stuff we see advertised all around us. Many of the things that seem to be "Must Have", end up quickly as just another unsatisfying "So What?" gathering dust in the garage!

Nothing is rustproof. Jesus warned about moths, thieves and rust that will *damage, destroy* and *depreciate* all the temporary things of this world. So many things we buy are actually of little benefit to us in the long term and can't bring us true contentment. If they could, you'd only need one CD, or one new dress and so on. But we get bored with that latest acquisition so soon don't we?

God says "You can ask me for what you need," but that does not mean we're always going to be harping on about things we want. Ask him instead to help you be content, then you're well on the way to being truly prosperous.

How prosperous are you?

When I ask people that question, most think about their bank balance, or take a quick inventory of the goods they have around the house. What came to your mind? Did you think in terms of diamonds, the car you drive or a get-rich-quick scheme?

There is a lot of talk about prosperity in certain church circles these days. A friend from Nigeria told me that an over-emphasis on material prosperity is, in his mind, the greatest threat to the real good news of the gospel in his country. Many preachers no longer talk about holiness but money.

While biblical prosperity does include having enough money to do what God has called you to do, it also includes having good health, peace of mind, good relationships, and much more. This is the picture of a person who experiences *shalom*, the blessing of God.

The apostle John wrote, *"I pray that you may prosper in all things and be in health, just **as your soul prospers.**"* [30] Biblical prosperity is multi-faceted! God measures prosperity in terms of how we are doing in spirit, soul, and body. Until we get hold of that, we have little to offer the world.

I met a man in Kenya who lived in a tiny hut. Edward had a few chickens, a little piece of ground, a wife, a couple of children, and a number of others – orphans – he had adopted. He wore a very old T-shirt, tatty jeans and no shoes. It might seem to you at first glance and according to Western standards that he lived in a state of poverty, but as I talked with him and he smiled broadly, I could see that he couldn't imagine being more prosperous!

Another man I know lives in a huge home on acres of land. He owned his own business and took early retirement. He had a fleet of cars, many of which stayed under covers to keep the dust off and never got the fast drive they were built for! He had a lovely wife, two children, was known in all the right circles, took his big boat out regularly around the Mediterranean, and played golf a great deal.

Judging from appearances, you'd say he was more prosperous than the first man. But when he opened up about his inner struggles, his fears and feelings of insecurity, his loneliness, lack of true friends and what I can only describe as soul sadness, I soon had my doubts.

Contrary to popular opinion, true prosperity does not come from having large sums of money, from stocks and shares, or from possessing an abundance of this world's treasures. None of those things impress the God of heaven and earth. Someone who is prosperous in God's eyes is rich because of his or her spiritual condition. It has little to do with material possessions. It has everything to do with your relationship with God and your love for the people he gives you to love.

Similarly, poverty is not the result of a poor financial state. In reality, poverty is a destructive spirit that robs people of relationships and dreams. Poverty of spirit is the curse of the Western world. It saps the joy of life, keeping people living lives limited by stinginess, as frustrated and unfulfilled they hoard all kinds of stuff that one day will be junk (unless it's really good when it may be sold as an antique). Solomon, who had plenty of money, observed:

> *"I have seen a grievous evil under the sun:*
> *wealth hoarded to the harm of its owner."* [31]

You've seen that too.

Ask

Jesus says it three ways . . .

> **Ask** and you will receive,
> **Seek** and you will find,
> **Knock** and the door will be opened.

None of this is automatic. We have our own part to play too. Jesus invites us to ask – and to see how God will answer. God can get some amazing deals! Whenever I can, I make sure I pray before I pay. Sometimes in prayer I realise I don't really need this purchase at all. Often there have been times I've prayed and seen a bill reduced, a discount offered, and a need met. This is because I was specific (and sometimes pretty desperate)!

On one occasion I asked a man for some help over a need that the church had. He was not a Christian, and had nothing to gain from helping. Eventually he said, "Why should I?" Good question.

I prayed for wisdom for a good answer, and I still don't know why I said it, but the words came out, "I am a blessed man. God has promised to bless those who bless me. If you bless me, I believe God will bless you." The guy agreed to help!

Another time a man who is not a believer approached me and said, "You know I don't believe in God?"

"Yes, I know you don't believe in God, David."

"Good, because if there was God I think he would want me to say to you that I am to pay for you to fly out to go anywhere you want to go in the world."

Interestingly, I'd just been praying that day that God would provide for me to visit some dear friends in Canada. As far as I'm aware David would still say he doesn't believe, but he paid!

The Bible says in James 4:2 (NKJV), *"you do not **have** because you do not **ask**"*. In 2 Kings 4, the prophet Elisha met a widow who had a great financial need. Put yourself in her shoes. In that culture she'd have her children taken away if she could not pay her debts. She's powerless, has no connections, no credit, no clout. What does she have? Just a small amount of oil. Elisha tells her to collect as many empty jars as she can from her neighbours. She's told she must *ask for many, not just a few*. She starts to pour the oil into the jars and has to keep on pouring until all the jars are full and her need is met.

The fact is, God is most honoured when we believe he's good enough to provide. He wants us to *ask not just for a few things*, but for *everything* we need. Our children ask us for things without worrying where the money will come from. It's their father's job to provide for them, isn't it?

I heard of one Dad having a family portrait photograph taken who said he wanted his kids to put their hands in *his* pockets, so it would look more natural! We need to have the same attitude. We have permission to ask our Father, for him to decide and provide. Look through the Bible and you'll see Jesus never worried about having his needs met. He didn't go to the bank, but down at the river bank he told Peter to get some money out of a fish's mouth! Jesus charged everything to his Father's credit card.

Next time you start to worry whether there is enough, adequate, sufficient – take a walk out in the world. Look at the stars. God has massive resources! And although he isn't there to meet our *greeds*, the God you can call Father promises to meet our *needs* if we ask.

Sow some seed

If you have a need – sow a seed. A farmer looking at an empty field doesn't just moan about it. He knows what the answer is. He has some seed. He doesn't hoard the seed, he's a fool if he eats the seed, so he sows it.

The Bible has a lot to say about the principle of sowing and reaping. You have to sow a seed, and sow generously. If you do sow you can *expect* to reap generously. If you don't sow, you mustn't expect to reap. There'll be no harvest. This is a very important, major key to mastering the art of living the better life Jesus promised.

Proverbs 10:22 (NKJV) says, *"The blessing of the LORD makes one rich..."* – that's the key to the kind of prosperity I'm talking about. When you seek God first in every area of your life, he will bless you and make you truly rich. How? Because you will be connected closely to him and you can know him now as your sin-removing, burden-bearing, problem-solving, generously providing, prayer-answering, truth-revealing, joy-restoring, life-giving, poverty-defeating, prosperity-granting Father God!

He will make you richer than a millionaire by making his presence more and more real in your life! That is valuable forever.

True prosperity is so much more than money! You can prosper in every area of your life as you grow spiritually – that is God's plan for you. The God you get to call Father desires that you would be able to say, "I am a man or a woman who is blessed by God." He wants you to be confident because you know that he will supply everything you need – and even enable you to pass your prosperity on to your descendants. There's a rich person for you!

I went to the bank the other day. The lady behind the counter asked me if I would like details of some super-duper new account they had just started. I smiled and said, "No thank you, I'm happy."

Now that must be something she doesn't hear every day, or else she was looking at what was in my account and wondered what I had to smile about! She looked at me quizzically and said, "You're *happy?*"

As I stood there and thought about all the blessings God had poured richly into my life, that I could never earn, work for or deserve, I smiled even broader, which seemed only to make her doubt my sanity more, and declared, "No, actually, I am *very* happy. I am the happiest man you will get in here today! I'm a prosperous man." Godliness with contentment is great gain.

Since I left the police force, many new laws will have been introduced, and some of the laws I used to work under and enforce will have been scrapped. However there are physical laws like the law of gravity that are here to stay. There are spiritual and universal laws also that will never change because they're not based on the whims of society, or the will of men, but on the Word of God. These principles are hard-wired into the very fabric of creation. They're part of how the universe *is* and operates.

The universal law says *you reap what you sow.* And you also reap *how* your sow. This operates in every area of your life, not just money. Miserly sowing brings in a miserable return. The sensible farmer doesn't hoard his seed, he knows he has to plant it, if he's going to get a harvest.

One of the richest men who ever lived said,

> "Cast your bread upon the waters,
> For you will find it after many days." [32]

Look how Eugene Peterson translates that:

> "Be generous: Invest in acts of charity.
> Charity yields high returns." [33]

Application? If you're going to get a harvest, you have to plant a seed. Invest in someone else, because when you're just wrapped up in yourself, that makes a pretty small package.

Honesty

We need to act with integrity over what we're given *and* what we give. Jesus said, "If God can trust us with the small things he will trust us with great things." If we are honest and generous, God keeps his hands on our finances. If we try to help ourselves out by not acting with integrity, he takes his hands off.

What kind of thing am I talking about here?

Well it applies to things like taxes, where we should ensure we are not paying too much, but be careful to pay what's *due*. Not too much, and not too little. This also involves expense claims, paper money or paper from the office. If we are dishonest in small things, eventually that sin will grow and trip or catch up with us, as it did with Judas.

The small things are big things to God. One of the Bible's most salutary tales is of an Israelite foot soldier by the name of Achan, who held onto some spoils of war and many men died as a result. Eventually he lost his whole family and his own life! [34]

It's the little things we have to watch. The Bible says the little foxes spoil the vineyard. A man I know told how God challenged him not to say his teenager was a child – she'd only just turned thirteen and they could have got away with it – so they could get a discount at a theme park. He said he figured the price of his integrity was not a couple of pounds!

While we're talking about being honest to God in the area of our finances, I need to say a quick word about tithing.

The twenty-two-year-old new Embassy World Snooker champion Shaun Murphy shocked many when he won the prestigious title in May 2005. However in a recent interview the Christian champ said that part of the reason for a reversal of fortunes was that he made the decision to tithe income to his local church.

Tithing simply means giving a tenth of all the finances God has given us back to God by giving to the church where we belong. In a recent service I gave a random congregation member £10. Then I asked for £1 back. The principle was explained, and that was a good day in church for that visitor!

If you're a follower of the Master of the way of the full life, you'll do this gladly after recognising all he's done for you, all he's given you. If the idea still strikes you as weird, don't let it put you off finding out more about Jesus. He doesn't need your money and he's more interested in getting your heart than your wages.

John Ortberg talks about tithing being like training wheels on a bicycle. That's because it's a kind of a test God puts to us as a minimum amount to learn how to be generous. And the wonderful thing is that God *also* says we can test *him* in it!

God promises that if you will trust him and be faithful to give ten per cent back of all he's given you to your local church community, he will bless you far more with the 90% that's left!

Self-help experts like Anthony Robbins and "Rich Dad" Richard Kiyosaki insist that financial freedom starts when you give away ten percent of your income. That's not because it's in the Bible, they just know the principle works!

I believe whether you are a Christian now or you're still a seeker (thanks for sticking with me) you can test God in this way! He has given you permission to in the Bible! [35] Why not try this for, say, six months? Give ten per cent of all your income faithfully to God's work in a local Bible believing church. See what God does with the ninety per cent.

So tithing is not giving. It's just *obeying* a spiritual principle. After that, generosity starts.

In 2 Corinthians 8, Paul wrote to that church in Corinth about a promise *they* had made. They said they would give an offering to the struggling Church of Jerusalem. He reminded them that although they've talked a good gift, *they haven't actually given anything yet*! He urges them not to let fear hold them back from fulfilling their promise to give to God's work.

You can tell Paul was pretty serious because he lets them know that he has sent his associate Titus and two other guys to collect the gift saying that they should be prepared for their arrival. This was the New Testament equivalent of sending the boys round! It's clear that Paul is not just asking them to give if they've had a good month, or if they feel like it. If we did that we might wait for ever.

Seriously, Paul encouraged them to be disciplined in their generosity and he urges them to give cheerfully. I recently had the great pleasure of getting to know TV comedian Tommy Cannon. When he spoke with an audience member at a recent outreach event at my church, he asked, "Are you having a good time?"

Having received a nod in return, Tommy shouted, "Well tell your face then!"

The Greek word for "cheerful" here is *hilaros* and means "with a happy face". The Lord loves a "hilarious" giver. It doesn't honour God when someone gives with a face like a bulldog licking a thistle. God wants you to give back from all he's given you, with a *happy* face! God wants us to give on the same basis that he has given to us: freely, abundantly and gladly. Before you count what you give, count your blessings. Having received so much love, don't you want to give something back to him?

In this passage [36] written to stir up the Corinthians, Paul talks about the Macedonian churches and what they are going through. He talks about, *"the most severe trial"* and *"extreme poverty"*. But he adds that despite this, their *"overflowing joy welled up in rich generosity"*.

Let me paraphrase. They gave ... **big time**. They pleaded for the privilege of being able to do so. Why and how did they do this? It was because *"they gave themselves first to the Lord"*.[37] Years ago I heard a story of a little girl who went and sat in the offering plate. That's the picture!

My friend, you might be reading this and financial fear has its talons digging in deep. You're thinking you just can't see any way to being free from the financial constraints that bind you. There are so many outgoings, how can we ever make room for another one?

Listen. God knows all your financial commitments. You can trust his promises, you can be free from fear. Begin to see what he sees. He wants you to be free to receive enough out of his abundance so that you can be generous on every occasion!

Let me encourage you with this thought. *You are already a very generous person.* I know that, because you're going to give away *all* your money! *Eventually* you're going to give away *100% of everything* you have on earth.

You picked up this book and thought you were going to read about how to *get* in this chapter. Now you discover it's about giving – and maybe you didn't realise that was where I was headed and you want to close the book. Please hold on!

The least I can do?

You might be thinking, *"I'm not giving it away."* But God is saying, "Well you're certainly not bringing it with you!" Eventually, we all give away *everything* we own. Just think about that. I talk to people so often who have the attitude to giving that says, "What's the bottom line? The bare minimum? How little can I give – and still have God happy with me and blessing me? Okay I have to give *some*, but what's the least I can get away with and still have God smiling when he looks at me?"

Be honest. You wondered didn't you? Why is that?

C.S. Lewis' brilliant book *The Screwtape Letters* is a work of fiction. It's a series of hellish memos – training letters from a senior demon called Uncle Screwtape to his nephew, a junior demon by the name Wormwood. It reveals in a humorous way how the enemy of our soul operates to blind us from the truth, in particular the truth about God and ourselves. Let me quote from it:

> "The sense of ownership in general is always to be encouraged. The humans are always putting up claims to ownership, which sound equally funny in heaven and hell, and we must keep them doing so.
>
> And all the time, the joke is that the word, 'mine' in its fully possessive sense cannot be uttered by a human being about anything. In the long run, our father or the enemy will say, 'mine', of each thing that exists, and especially, of each man."

It has been said that there is in fact nothing in all creation of which God does not say, "Mine." So from an eternal perspective, any time you or I say, "that's mine," about *anything*, it sounds daft. The angels certainly get to giggling over that.

If you think you're an owner maybe you need to look around your home and take a full inventory. I hope you'll realise, *"I'm going to give this all away one day, **I don't get to keep any of it.**"* It's not yours. Even your best stuff might not outlast you. Don't bother writing your name on this book. Give it to someone else! It's not really yours. You would do well to have the joy of giving your children some of their inheritance early. I dedicated this book to my Dad who died this year. Before he died I remember he gave me his favourite pair for "Ray Ban" sunglasses – I think he was starting to get the picture.

What we do with our money and possessions is *a test*, according to Jesus. It doesn't matter how good a person we think we are, whether we're kind to old ladies and grow our own vegetables. It doesn't matter how loud we sing in the choir or how much Bible we know.

Jesus has a better test:

" . . . *where your treasure is, there your heart will be also.*" [38]

And you know that's true. You spend your dosh on the things you care about.

Why do so many churches and ministries limp along and make do? Do you know how much ministry you can do with £5? About £5 worth. Isn't it funny how the note that looks so small in Tescos looks so big when the plate comes round in church? You hold onto your money because you think you own it. But if you can get quiet enough, you'd hear heaven laughing. And hell laughs louder.

Stewards R Us

At the end of our lives we'll all discover the truth: we don't really own *anything*. If you own it, you'd take it with you wherever you go. We're stewards. What's a steward? A steward simply manages what belongs to another. That's you. You might be a good steward or a bad one, but you're looking after some of God's stuff right now. One day he'll ask what you did with it, and that's not because he doesn't know. This is what the Bible calls being held to account.

God has loaned to you, for a *short* amount of time, some money and other things. You are responsible and accountable for your stewardship of it. Now you don't need me to tell you what a good steward does do you? In Britain I'd only have to mention the names Robert Maxwell or Nick Leeson, or perhaps in other parts of the world to talk about Enron and you'll know that a bad steward just does what he wants with stuff that belongs to another.

A good steward looks to the owner and says, "Thank you for trusting me with this, now what do you want me to do with it?" A good steward protects, cares for, invests and grows the owner's assets.

God your heavenly Father has given so much to you. *You're a steward*. God has put on loan with us certain wealth, assets, talents etc. So he has every right to ask what you are going to do with **his** stuff. You don't own it. You don't have to worry and fret and be in fear over it. God has promised to provide for your needs as you steward his stuff.

Think now about how much God has given you, say, this week, this month, this year. Throughout your life in terms of money, gifts, blessings, jobs and connections all are opportunities you got from him. Here's my question. *How much out of all he's given you are you willing to give back to him?* Everything you have came from God. He's given it to you, and now you decide, will you act like an owner of it, or a steward?

Exercise

Give something today.

Uh-oh...

Yes, I'm talking money.

Today (don't put it off) – *give*.

Write a cheque to a mission or development agency working with the poor. Push some money through the door of someone you know is in need. Ask God what he, the owner, wants you, the steward, to do with it.

Give it. With a happy face. Today. It's not your money.

Set yourself free from fear over finances by sowing a seed of generosity! This book should cost more than you thought it would when you finish it, or you're not doing it right, and the principles in it won't work for you because you're not applying them. You have some money God has given you, how much will you give back to him today as you steward the rest? Freedom from fear over finances never starts by getting another credit card. It won't get better by consolidating your loans into that latest deal with the nice smiling people on daytime TV.

No. It starts when you decide to *give yourself first to the Lord*. Put yourself on the plate, then he'll have your money too. You won't have fear over finances – but you'll *abound* in every good work. Why settle for less than God's plan?

Take that to the bank!

*"God is able to make all grace abound to you,
so that in all things at all times,
having all that you need,
you will abound in every good work."* [39]

I Don't Have to Be Afraid to Die

"Hope I die before I get old..."
(The Who)

"I hope I'm old before I die."
(Robbie Williams)

A merchant in Baghdad sent his servant to market to buy provisions. A little while later the servant came back, white and trembling., "Master," he said, "just now when I was in the marketplace I was jostled by a woman in the crowd and when I turned I saw it was Death that jostled me. She looked at me and made a threatening gesture. Now, lend me your horse, and I will ride away from this city to avoid my fate. I will go to Samarra, so that Death will not find me."

The merchant lent him his horse and the servant mounted it, dug his spurs in its flanks and he went as fast as the horse could gallop. Then the merchant went down to the marketplace and he saw Death standing in the crowd. He came to Death and said, "Why did you make a threatening gesture to my servant when you saw him this morning?"

"That was not a threatening gesture, Death said, "It was only a start of surprise. I was astonished to see him in Baghdad, for I had an appointment with him tonight in Samarra." [40]

We all have an appointment in Samarra. Some day, our meeting with death will come. Death is the one thing that we will all share in common. The Greek poet Euripedes said, "Death is the debt we all must pay." All of us.

The Bible says, "No one can keep from dying or put off the day of death." [41]

That is a battle we cannot escape; we cannot cheat our way out.

Death is a frightening thing isn't it? The next item on my "Don't have to do" list, is that I don't have to be afraid of death. Yet to get to that place I have to look it in the face, and be honest about my feelings towards it.

Francis Bacon wrote, "Men fear death, as children fear to go in the dark." I remember as a small boy long nights lying in bed when I would cry because of the irrational fear that my parents would die and I'd be left alone. That was more difficult for me than facing my own mortality; to lose someone.

The word used is "bereaved". It's rooted in an old English word that means "robbed". That's how it feels. Ask the mother robbed of her baby. Question the man robbed of his wife after a car crash. Listen to those standing in casualty after hearing the news they dreaded. Robbed.

Death is the last taboo subject of society. The one thing you really shouldn't discuss in polite company. Yet the two main jobs I've worked at have made me very familiar with death.

I saw my first dead body when I was sixteen. A desperate young woman took the awful option of suicide by placing herself in the way of a train. I've seen murder victims including a mother who in some moment of unexplainable madness tried to kill her three children by pouring petrol on them and setting fire to them. She was only stopped when her eldest daughter of fourteen years of age picked up a knife and stabbed her mother to protect her sisters.

I still shudder as I remember helping carry bodies off the plane at the Manchester Airport Disaster in 1985. Fifty-five people, men women and children, were trapped inside the burning 737 on the runway. This week as I write, the news is full of two hundred deaths as terrorists struck. Many of still can't get our heads around a Beslan, much less a tsunami.

But it's not just the shocking deaths and disasters that are frightful is it? I've sat and held hands with countless grieving families as they've told me about a child who died, or a mother, a father, husband or wife. Time and again I recognised the look on their faces that says, "The world has just changed totally for us. We don't know what to do with our shock and pain. How can *we* go on – now he's gone?"

> Stop all the clocks, cut off the telephone,
> Prevent the dog from barking with a juicy bone,
> Silence the pianos and with muffled drum
> Bring out the coffin, let the mourners come.

Let aeroplanes circle moaning overhead
Scribbling on the sky the message He Is Dead,
Put crepe bows round the white necks of the public doves,
Let the traffic policemen wear black cotton gloves.

He was my North, my South, my East and West,
My working week and my Sunday rest,
My noon, my midnight, my talk, my song;
I thought that love would last for ever: I was wrong.

The stars are not wanted now: put out every one;
Pack up the moon and dismantle the sun;
Pour away the ocean and sweep up the wood.
For nothing now can ever come to any good.[42]

Stop all the clocks. Some of these people shake a fist toward heaven, others open their hands for help. Frankly I don't know how anyone who is not closely connected to God copes at times like this.

So, what do we do with death? What do you do? What do you think happens next? Last time I checked, the mortality rate was still running at 100%. People have developed a number of strategies to cope with the ultimate statistic:

▶ **Ignore death**

"There is no error, no sin sickness, nor death."

Mary Baker Eddy, founder of the Christian Science cult, wrote that – just before she died.

Wittgenstein wrote,

"Death is not an event in life. It is not a fact in the world."

Really? Come and check out my church graveyard. The man who invented crosswords is buried there. (As you come in from the car park he's six down and ten across.)

The apostle Paul reminds the church at Corinth of a saying current in his day, *"Eat and drink, for tomorrow we die . . . "* If this life is all there is, then that's probably the best advice available. Spend up your maximum credit limit, eat all you can, drink all you can. Live for today, because that's all you've got.

We all know we're not immune to death, but if we push it to the back of our minds, maybe it won't happen to us – will it? Life is brief, futile and pretty insignificant. You might as well make the best of a bad lot because you only go round once.

Which leads us on nicely to the next strategy.

▶ Get mystical

We're just part of the circle of life, according to Elton John and the great theologians in the *Lion King*. You're no better or worse than any other animal. When you die, you feed the worms. Maybe you'll have come back as one of them anyway, or a bird that eats the worms, or something like that. Maybe you'll come back as a ghost, or a spirit, or a butterfly or a wave of the sea, or a star in the sky.

And you were Cleopatra in a previous life, so who knows what you'll be in the next?

▶ Be morbid

I once had someone tell me that when they lost someone it was like there was a very sharp stone inside their stomach. It cut deeply and unexpectedly pretty much all the time. But then as the weeks and months turned into years, the edges of the stone wore off, though they still knew they'd feel the weight of it. That's normal and natural. There's no one way to grieve that will be right for everyone. And there's no set time on anything.

But some people seem to sharpen the stone themselves. They're resigned to living a life as if death was all there is. They carry a shroud wherever they go. For all sorts of reasons, they *can't* or *won't* move on.

Our culture feeds the death obsession. You meet young people (usually dressed all in black) who seem to celebrate death and destruction through some of the music they listen to and the art they celebrate. But talking to them, it isn't because they've found any answer. It's a mask to hide their fear. Despair. The truth is they're scared – scared to death.

Lars Ulrich, drummer with the heavy metal band Metallica says, "The thing I've been unable to control, in my quest to control everything around me, is death."

▶ Deny we can know anything about death

People who don't know the reality of the resurrection of Christ will say, "Dead men tell no tales. No-one ever died and came back to tell us about it." I meet well meaning people all the time who'll say, "Nobody knows *anything* for sure." The obvious rejoinder? "You seem pretty sure about that."

Sometimes people can try a pseudo-intellectual approach like this, "We should all keep searching for answers, as long as nobody ever says they've come to a definite conclusion." To be considered really intelligent it seems you have to remain ignorant about all the most important questions!

Surely to stay in the tunnel of agnosticism is like making your house in the Channel Tunnel. It's alright as a place to go through on a journey, but you wouldn't want to try to live there.

▶ *Laugh it off*

Some people try to face death with a grin. Mark Twain famously declared when he heard of someone's death, "I didn't attend the funeral, but I sent a nice letter saying I approved of it." Woody Allen said, "I don't want to achieve immortality through my work. I want to achieve it through not dying." Somerset Maugham said, "Death is a very dull, dreary affair, and my advice to you is to have nothing whatsoever to do with it." Easier said than done, I'm afraid.

And try as I might to force a laugh, I would remain afraid, afraid of death, if these were the only options to deal with it.

▶ *Sentimentalise it*

There are various forms this can take. Sometimes it's a Christian who refuses to mourn because of their mistaken belief they'd be letting God down if they didn't keep on smiling, even at the graveside. They forget that Jesus wept at the tomb of a friend. The true Christian view of death is to recognise and accept that it really is a hideous thing; our enemy and the last enemy of God.[43]

We don't cut short the grieving process by not facing and dealing with the pain of the loss. The cult of Christian Science just denies the existence of death, pain and disease, and I have heard some preachers who seem to have got half way toward that position too.

The most important thing for Christians in the face of death is not to show that we have hope beyond the grave (though we do) but to be *real* this side of it. Other people want to cover the whole affair in flowers, so that the reality of what has happened doesn't hit home. Boxer Joe Louis said, "Everybody wants to go to heaven, but nobody wants to die." And as we lay the flowers we write the card expressing the conviction that this person, like everyone else, will be in heaven now.

I remember one sympathy card that read, "We all started out the same way and we'll all end up the same way." In theological terms this is called universalism. It is common currency these days and it means that if you're sincere, no matter what you believe, or refuse to believe, no matter what you do or don't do, you too will end up in heaven. God has to let you in – that's his job. Well, we have to look at that more closely.

Two best selling novels I've read in the last couple of weeks reveal something of the fascination of our culture with death. Both are good stories, and operate from that same basic premise, everyone gets to heaven. *The Five People You Meet in Heaven* by Mitch Albom, soon to be a feature film starring Jon Voight, contains some important lessons about life. But what it tries to teach about death and what comes after flies in the face of what God has told us about those matters in the Bible.

The Lovely Bones is a kind of spiritual detective story with a young girl who's a murder victim now in heaven, and again it's a great read. But like the film *Ghost* it starts out from the premise that it doesn't matter what you believe about God, he's benignly irrelevant and operating a wide-open door policy. Unless of course you're "a bad person".

But who draws that particular line?

Our culture has embraced without thinking too deeply about it (because they can't really bear to?) a mixture of wishful thinking together with the cynicism of atheistic philosophers; like Voltaire, who spent his life taking pot-shots at religion but died with a desperate groan. One atheist's gravestone bears the words, "All dressed up, and nowhere to go."

Albert Camus said, "Death is philosophy's only problem." He was an atheist and admitted that atheism can offer no comfort in the face of death. You see, everything we do includes some kind of hope. However, what kind of hope can the atheist give in the face of a meaningless life that ends meaninglessly?

Jean-Paul Sartre declared that death is non-threatening provided we view it in the third person. It isn't until we face the first person, "*I* am going to die, *my* death," that death becomes threatening. Most people never assume first person attitudes to death during their life.

So again I need to ask you – *what about you*? Where is the belief system you have about life and death and the afterlife taking you? Make no mistake, it *is* taking you somewhere. The test of a belief system or way of dealing with death is not just in how you live it out, but in whether it outlives *you*.

Does it deal with the truth about death? Are you ready for the Bible's Truth about Death?

The choices we make now make all the difference

Remember Russell Crowe encouraging his troops in *Gladiator*? "What we do in life echoes in eternity."

In the film *Braveheart* William Wallace declares, "Every man dies. Not every man really lives."

I don't think any of us are really ready to live until we're ready to die. The phone rang in the middle of writing these words. Yet again it was the local undertaker, it's never good news with him. What will this next funeral be like? Before I'd finished editing the chapter, another call, a church member's mother just died.

I remember sitting in the car with a friend who never seemed quite ready to commit his life to Christ "just yet", though he always had the most interesting questions. He put his hand on my shoulder and then looked me in the straight in the eye before he asked me, "In your experience, do Christians face death better than those who are not Christians?"

I thought a while before answering. I wanted to tell the truth, as clearly as I knew how.

"I have no doubt that those I have known with the greatest assurance and security about death are free to live with the least amount of panic when they know they are going to die."

Let me give you an illustration of that. These days you don't need a travel agent to book a holiday, you can do it on the internet. We've done that for our holiday this year. But Zoë doesn't relax until she knows we have the tickets. Holding the ticket means you're getting on the plane. Then you can rest assured.

And you want to double check that they got the destination right don't you?

Let me stretch the analogy. When you've had the ticket, got on the plane, and finally arrived at the destination, you can see the difference in the arrivals lounge between people who have someone pre-arranged to meet them, compared with people who have made no such arrangement.

To be met with a smile and an embrace, to see people being picked up and kissed and celebrated – I love to see that at airport arrivals. I loved watching the end or the film *Love Actually* for the same reason. It's a picture for me of heaven and the way we who know Christ *now* will be welcomed by him *then*.

According to Scripture, however many philosophies or systems people come up with to deal with it, whether they deny it, celebrate it, come up with a plan to put it off or laugh it off, humanity is not divided up into many different camps on this issue. Only two.

Two categories

While we're talking about films, can I remind you about *Titanic*? The most successful film in movie history. A major theme you'll recall is the difference between classes, the distinction between the rich and the poor.

On a recent trip back to my home town of Manchester my family and I visited the *Titanic* exhibition, where you could see many of the actual artefacts, what the cabins were like and so on.

There were some passengers on the first-class deck, and there were those down below, down through second- and third-class all the way to steerage. The film plays with and highlights the differences between the famous and the not so famous, the young and the old, the haves and the have-nots, from Lord Astor down to people being checked for fleas.

On the *Titanic* there were all kinds of distinctions; immigrants and non-immigrants, rich and poor, servants and served. All looking up or down at each other or looking sideways. And the love interest is Kate Winslet's rich girl meets Leonardo DiCaprio's poor boy.

As I entered the exhibition they gave us all tickets with the name of one of the real voyagers on it, someone who was a passenger that fateful night. All the family got a name, and we all checked a list as we left. I was the only one who "died" (I suppose it's just my luck). James Cameron said, "The *Titanic* is a metaphor of the inevitability of death. We're all on the *Titanic*."

When the *Titanic* sank, newspapers worldwide printed two columns side by side. Ultimately, only one distinction now mattered. One column said, "Those *saved*" the other said "Those *lost*". The two eternal categories. Saved and lost.

Saved and lost

The great nineteenth-century entury preacher Charles Spurgeon once urged his hearers to spend time thinking about this issue and after his sermon he asked them to go home from the meeting and write down on a piece of paper which of those two camps they fell into. "Just write one word, saved or lost."

One man was so incensed by the suggestion that not everyone got to heaven, he determined to go home and write the word "lost" to spite the preacher and the God he claimed to speak for. At home, raging as he sat at his desk, he pulled out his pen to write that word. His young daughter sensing what was in his eyes and heart, saw that he had already formed the letter "L".

His little girl begged him, "No Daddy, don't write that word! Ask God to save you. Ask Jesus to save you!"

The man wrestled with himself for a moment before seeing the love God had for him reflected in his little girl's eyes. He broke down in tears and asked God to forgive him, save him and lead his life, from that day on and for eternity.

I don't know how many people will be saved by Jesus. One day some people came and asked the Master of the full life that question about life ever after. He answered them simply by saying, "Never mind about them, what about you? Make sure you enter by the narrow gate." [44]

No-one, no matter how rich, famous, good or successful in this short life, can get victory over death by himself. It's the great leveller isn't it? We can climb to the top of all sorts of ladders, but there's only one man who stepped out of his own grave – and can lead us out too. To handle death, we need to know the one who defeated it.

The fact is, outside of a relationship with Jesus Christ, there is no hope for a cure for your terminal illness, the disease of death we're all suffering from. If God speaks to you and points that out, it is not because he doesn't love you. He's like a doctor who has to tell you the diagnosis before you will accept the treatment, so he can deal with it. He would do you no favours by not hurting your feelings.

God knows death is an enemy. Death is *your* enemy. Death is inescapable, inevitable and permanent; it cost so much for the victory over it to be won, and God wants you to share in that victory too. Your choice makes all the difference, and there are only two categories.

> **Choose now. The time is right.**
> **You don't get a second chance to make the right choice.**

Whatever reincarnationists might want to believe, they'll discover when this life ends that you don't get just back on the merry-go-round. The Bible says in Hebrews 9:27 *"it is appointed for men to die **once**, but after this the judgment."*

Rick Warren says that because God loves us, he's told us in advance what the questions will be you'll have to answer when you stand there before him:

- "What did you do with my Son, Jesus?"
- "What did you do with the time I gave you?"

The time to make your choice is shorter than you think.

It is said that Satan once called to him all the emissaries of hell and declared he wanted to send one of them to earth to help women and men in the ruination of their souls. He asked which one would want to go. One creature came forward and said, "I will go."

Satan said, "If I send you, what will you tell the children of Adam?"

He said, "I will tell them there is no heaven."

Satan said, "They will not believe you, for our enemy has placed eternity in their hearts. You may not go."

Another came forward, darker and fouler than the first. Satan said, "If I send you, what will you tell the children of Adam?"

He said, "I will tell them there is no hell."

Satan looked at him and said, "Oh, no; they will not believe you, for in every human heart there's a thing called conscience, an inner voice which testifies to the truth that not only will good be triumphant, but that evil will be defeated. You will not go."

One last creature came forward from the darkest place of all. Satan said to him, "And if I send you, what will you say to women and men to aid in the destruction of their eternal souls?"

He said, "I will tell them there is no hurry."

Satan said, "Go!"

The question is not, *"Will* I live forever?" Everyone lives forever. The real question is, *"Where* will you live forever?" *"Where* will you spend eternity?" It all rises and falls (and you will rise or fall) depending on what you have done with Jesus Christ, who died and now lives so you also can live.

On 15 April 1989, ninety-six fans were crushed to death in the Hillsborough football stadium in Sheffield, another two hundred were injured. At one of the hospitals where victims were taken, a surgeon spoke to the parents who had come to find out the fate of their children. He read the names of those killed and expressed his sympathy. In trying to bring comfort he said that he believed that God understood the parents' grief and was with them in their time of need. One father bitterly responded: "What does God know about losing a son?"

The first time I went to see *The Passion of the Christ*, I was stunned by its depiction of the horrors of the cross. Like many who have seen it, I was literally speechless at the end. So often we skip through the familiar passages that talk about the suffering, torture and agonising death of Jesus. The cross has lost its shock value. It was a curse, shameful.

God knows about losing a Son. God knows about death – and Jesus has conquered it! At one point in the film, I was beginning to despair, my heart felt like it was literally breaking as I watched all that Christ went through for me and you.

Just when I was feeling angry at the religious leaders who lied and betrayed, the soldiers who enjoyed hurting him so horribly, the film changed scene to another time; an earlier time, when Jesus said these words about his own impending death, *"No one takes* [my life] *from Me, but I lay it down of Myself. I have power to lay it down, and I have power to take it again."* [45]

And I know I'm not spoiling the end of the film for you when I say this same Christ steps out of the tomb still bearing the wounds of his love for us! Mel Gibson in an interview said, "Without the resurrection, our faith is dead. The story's not complete without it." That was the only way for death and sin to be conquered.

> "Fear not death, for the sooner we die the longer we shall be immortal."
>
> (Benjamin Franklin)

When preacher Donald Grey Barnhouse's first wife died from cancer she was only in her thirties. Dr Barnhouse bravely said he would preach at the funeral. As he drove his children to the church, he agonised, "How do I explain to them what has happened?"

On the way to the service a large truck passed by their car and cast its large shadow over them. He asked his children, "Would you rather be run over by that truck, or its shadow?"

His twelve-year-old daughter replied, "By the shadow, I suppose, a shadow can't hurt you."

Dr Barnhouse then turned to his children and said, "Your mother has not been overrun by death, but by the shadow of death." At her funeral service he preached on Psalm 23:4,

> *"Even though I walk*
> *through the valley of the shadow of death,*
> *I will fear no evil,*
> *for you are with me."*
>
> (NIV)

Where else can you find comfort in the face of death? Times without number I've seen this, as I've sat at hospital bedsides with dying people, or spoken to those left behind in a dingy crematorium. What a difference it makes to have faith in the risen Christ!

While older gravestones at my ancient church used to proclaim the hope of resurrection, these days they just say the person's name. They used to bury them facing east, to await the return and their physical resurrection. But now at the graveside so many people have no such hope, only fear; no light, only darkness.

How will they have any hope, unless we ourselves have it, and then bring it to them?

The greatest tragedy about death is that so many people do not know the one who chose death so we can choose life! Jesus "holds the keys of death and death's domain".[46]

How are they going to choose life, if they do not know the Prince of Life? Jesus died for our sins, and rose from the dead. Without that there is no hope. That is his victory, it is also our message. That is his triumph; it is our great assurance.

I heard a sociologist called Tony Campolo say that he had prayed with a man who was seriously ill with cancer on Sunday night. On Wednesday he got a phone call from the guy's wife. She reminded Tony that he had prayed for her husband who *had* cancer.

Tony thought, *"Had?* What happened!?"

Then she said, "He died today." Tony felt terrible, he expressed his sorrow to the man's wife, but her response amazed him.

"Don't feel bad. When he came into that church that Sunday he was filled with anger. He knew he was going to be dead in a short period of time and he hated God. He was fifty-eight years old and he wanted to see his children and grandchildren grow up. He was angry that this all-powerful God didn't take away his sickness and heal him. He would lie in bed and curse God. The more his anger grew towards God, the more miserable he was to everybody around him. It was an awful thing to be in his presence.

"After you prayed for him, a peace came over him and a joy came into him. Tony, the last three days have been the best days of our lives. We've sung. We've laughed. We've read Scripture. We prayed. Oh, they've been wonderful days. And I called to thank you for laying your hands on him and praying for healing."

Then she said something incredibly profound. She said, "He wasn't cured, but he was healed."

We followers of the way of full and eternal life, grieve. Oh yes. But not as those who have no hope, for we know the God who raises the dead. Death is not the end but the beginning. Those who choose life shall rise again to rule with Christ forever.

The poet and hymn writer George Herbert said, "Death used to be an executioner, but the gospel has made him just a gardener." Jesus rose from the dead! The shadow of death can't hurt us. If you surrender your life now to him, you don't have to ever be afraid of death.

As technology improves, maybe you will have some good replacement parts along the way, but one day I assure you the garage will say, "Sorry, we don't do that model anymore."

You have an appointment in Samarra. Only a fool would go all through life totally unprepared for something you know is inevitably going to happen. One day you're going to stand before God. Your life, too, is going to end.

God will ask you, "Did you really know my Son, Jesus Christ. He loved you, did you love him back?"

The choice matters. The only categories that are going to count are, Were you *saved* by Christ? Or, were you *lost* without Christ? No second chances then. So why not ask him now? Tell Jesus, "I want to get to know you. I want to put my faith in you and help lead others I know to you as well." Why don't you do that today and make a difference for eternity?

Ponder

- Why do you think people treat death as a taboo subject?
- How have you coped with losses in your own life – remember you don't have to have lost a close family member to experience grief.
- Do you agree with the observation that people with a strong faith in Christ may cope better with death than those who perhaps would describe themselves as agnostic?

Practical steps

- Confront the reality of death by comforting someone else who is grieving. Don't be afraid you'll say the wrong thing. Often just being there with a listening ear is the right thing.
- Visit a hospice or a cancer ward.

I Don't Have to Get Angry

"A little dog and a big dog are always fighting inside me," a man told his friend, "but I know the little dog will win."
"How do you know?"
"Because that's the one I feed."

"Of the Seven Deadly Sins, anger is possibly the most fun. To lick your wounds, to smack your lips over grievances long past, to roll over your tongue the prospect of bitter confrontations still to come, to savour to the last toothsome morsel both the pain you are given and the pain you are giving back – in many ways it is a feast fit for a king. The chief drawback is that what you are wolfing down is yourself. The skeleton at the feast is you." [47]

I can tell you from painful experience and not just observation, outbursts of anger cause a lot of trouble. It's only one letter short of "danger". As I look back over my years as a man who has often struggled with a slow brain, a fast mouth and a quick fuse, I remember having to make embarrassing and personally expensive apologies.

I recall losing friendships, or at least having them cool off. I remember awkward and uncomfortable silences around people I should have been happy to talk with most, because I love them best. No wonder Marcus Aurelius wrote, "How much more grievous are the consequences of anger than the causes of it."

People who struggle with anger find they don't appear on other's guest lists as often as they used to or would like to. These people have more difficulties at work. Look around their houses and you'll see things lying broken that they smashed to bits trying to repair. They're anxious, often depressed, especially if their anger is pushed down on the inside and burns like an acid, rather than being dealt with healthily.

And (whether they see it or refuse to), all around such people are others, battered and bruised, or walking on eggshells, just wishing and hoping for the day when they will change or die – or escape will come some other way.

Living in the war zone

"I once talked with a woman who was a teenager in Holland during World War II. 'Everything we did was under the shadow of the war,' she explained. 'Day and night – the war affected everything.' They woke up to the sounds of soldiers in the streets; they spent every waking hour wondering who would be arrested next; they went to sleep hungry because the soldiers had stolen their food. Living in the war zone affected every aspect of their lives."[48]

One day Alexander the Great, in a fit of rage, struck his favourite general, and killed him stone dead. This man was his best friend, Clitus. He cried out, "I've conquered the world. But I can't even conquer my own soul!" With that in mind how poignant to read Proverbs 16:32 (NIV) which declares,

> *"Better a patient man than a warrior,*
> *a man who controls his temper than one who takes a city."*

A problem with anger

I recall an appraisal talk with my colleague, friend and spiritual father Eric Delve. We sat by a roaring fire and as a good leader should he said lots of positive things before getting to what he really wanted to talk to me about. "Anthony, I think you have a problem with anger. I've seen it flare up in meetings sometimes."

Now of course I am a man of God and I didn't have a problem with anger. The very suggestion that I might have a problem caused my veins to bulge. My muscles tensed, my throat went dry and I wanted to shout, "What are you talking about!!?" I remember leaving the room half an hour later with one verse from the Bible ringing away in my head, a verse Eric had gently asked me to commit to memory:

> *". . . man's anger does not bring about the righteous life that God desires."*

> (James 1:20, NIV)

That's a categorical statement. Any time I get angry, I simultaneously short-circuit the purposes of God. I am so grateful Eric loved me enough to tell me the truth and help me confront that issue. *"Wounds from a friend can be trusted."* [49] I needed that. I need to be reminded of the fact that whenever I get angry, God effectively takes his hands off the situation and says, "Okay, have it *your* way." I'm not following the way of the Master of the abundant life any more, I'm going a different way.

I don't want that to happen. I don't want to drive this car called my life anymore. I often go too hard and fast and become a danger to others. I keep on crashing when I drive my life. So how is it possible to get a grip on anger?

The three "R"s

1. Remember

Remember you lose when you lose your temper. Will Rogers said, "People who fly into a rage always make a bad landing." Because God takes his hands off the situation and leaves you to it. His purposes won't be fulfilled while I'm angry. Every single time I lose my temper, there are negative consequences. Instead, as I remember the negative effects, that causes me to calm down.

2. Restrain

Restrain your remarks. You don't have to say everything that's on your mind when you're angry. You'll save a ton of grief if you *limit* your words and actions. You don't even have to attend every argument you get invited to.

3. Reflect

Think. Delay. There used to be a cheesy advert on TV that said, "Men can't help acting on impulse." But God can help you before you respond impulsively. Take a moment and a deep breath. Make time to calm down, cool down, delay. You can learn something about yourself and other people if you'll reflect on what was happening that made you lose your cool.

Let's look at these three anger-busters in more detail.

Remember ... you lose

My kids sometimes make an "L" shape and stick it on their foreheads, declaring someone or something a "LOSER!" Not very polite, but it gets the point home. Next time you let the fur fly and blow up in rage, put an "L" on your own head. You've become a loser.

An angry person makes poor decisions, wounds those he loves, overreacts, disciplines too severely, and does and says things that would never otherwise enter his head in calmer moments.

> *"A patient man has great understanding,*
> *but a quick-tempered man displays folly."* [50]

That means people with hot tempers do stupid things. So I get stuck behind someone driving too slowly and it gets me home five minutes later, is it really that big a deal? You can't change the situation. You need to change your reaction. Soccer genius Eric Cantona jumped into the stands to kick a fan who upset him. He lost everything for a moment of madness. When you lose your temper you always lose something else. You can lose respect, health, your job, your marriage partner and your kids. We all know a person that has happened to. Read the papers and you'll see rock stars, football managers, athletes and film idols that lose out by losing it.

> *"The fool who provokes his family to anger and resentment will finally have nothing worthwhile left."* [51]

You can lose a lot more than your temper.

Anger starts first in the family. Lots of us grow up around some very unhelpful models of how to deal with anger – and unless we recognise and renounce them, we're going to repeat the patterns of previous generations (show our kids the same thing with devastating effects).

But anger works!

Why do we lose our temper? We know why. Because it *works*. In the short term anyway. People change their behaviour, people do what you want. If they were nagging, now they shut up. They weren't listening till, like Alex Ferguson, you "hair-dryered" them. Well now you have their full attention. If they weren't driving very considerately, now they know from your hand signals how you feel about that kind of discourtesy. You might even find at work that getting angry sometimes gets you ahead of the pack. It works.

But not for long. When you shout and bawl (get angry) in order to "motivate" someone, most people will comply out of fear, but they always resent it. He who complies against his will, is of the same opinion still.

In the long run, you lose again. So, next time the adrenaline starts to pound through a little quicker, when your teeth start to clench, your muscles flex, and your hands start to tighten so they become more like fists; remember the results. Lose your temper, and you *will* lose out.

Restrain your response

Novelist Ambrose Bierce said, "Speak when you are angry and you will make the best speech you will ever regret." Having a sharp tongue is the quickest way to cut your own throat. Use sweet words, you may have to eat them. Your words can wind you up or cool you down, and of course they'll have that effect on the other party too.

> *"He who guards his mouth and his tongue*
> *keeps himself from calamity."* [52]

The problem is I sometimes find words come very easily when I'm angry. Sometimes I can think of the best, the most sarcastic and cutting thing to say when I've worked myself up a good head of steam. But in the end it hurts me too. I bet you've yelled sometimes and regretted it soon after? It's like a hand grenade, causing indiscriminate damage. Restrain your response. Pull the plug rather than pulling the pin.

> *"A gentle response **defuses** anger,*
> *but a sharp tongue kindles a temper-fire."* [53]

Anger is infectious! If you get it, you can easily give it to other people. It's contagious. You can kindle a temper-fire in others. I saw this a lot when policing at football matches where the crowd mentality kicks in. If you're around other people who have hot heads, watch out!

If somebody's continually angry at you, eventually you're likely to get angry at them. It is contagious. Remember the universal principle we looked at in Chapter 4? You reap what you sow. Sow harsh and angry words, you'll reap them back in spades. If you want soft words spoken to you, then you need to sow some soft words. Whatever you sow you'll reap. No one co-operates with someone who seems to be against them. We have to learn to establish a level of rapport before we'll get a positive outcome.

Red mist

When I feel the old red mist descend these days, I try to remember to pray that the Lord will help me *resist retaliation*. Harsh words only escalate the problem, taking it to a whole new level. Soft words tone down the tension. *"A gentle answer defuses anger."*

Whose anger does it defuse? Firstly yours. The more I vent my spleen and raise my voice, the angrier I get. To turn down the anger, I have to remember to turn down the volume and speak in a quieter tone.

There have been times when I've taken a deep breath and slowed the tone of my voice, to match the pace of the other person. Then slow it down further, using kind words and even an apology or to say, "I understand." I have been amazed how fast the wind comes out of the other person's sails when *I* stopped huffing and puffing!

It's a well known fact that children learn from the models that they observe. They're watching all the time for clues on how to deal with the world. If you are a parent like me, do you realise that every time you shout, throw something or swear, you're modelling how to deal with anger for your kids? "Kids, come and watch how Daddy deals with life's challenges!"

Every time you lose your temper you're teaching your children how to get angry.

I'm still trying to remember the lesson Eric reminded me of. My anger *does not* work the righteousness God requires. So there are things I don't do or say because however I handle anger, I'm showing my kids what to do.

People are like tubes of toothpaste. Whatever is inside you will come out when you get squeezed. Some people's emotional cups are filled right up to the brim with anger, stress, tension and hurt. When life's going along steadily, it all looks okay. But just a little squeeze or shake – and watch out! Anytime anyone or anything gives them a nudge – they spill. Lose it. Blow up. It doesn't take much, a little jostle maybe – and the people nearby get hurt.

That's why Jesus said,

> *"Take my yoke upon you and learn from me, for I am gentle and humble in heart, and you will find rest for your souls."* [54]

Reflect, before you (over)react

Thomas Jefferson said, "When you're angry you count to 10. When you're very angry, count to 100."

By way of contrast, Mark Twain said, "When angry count four; when very angry, swear!"

This is the big one for me. A lesson I'm beginning to learn is to think it through first. Not to respond impulsively. Instead I want to delay, defer, deliberate, reflect – before reacting.

Take the Bible's fool test:

> *"A fool gives full vent to his anger,*
> *but a wise man keeps himself under control."* [55]

The world's advice is to get a punchbag and let it all out. But one of the great remedies for anger is delay. Whatever you were going to do in the heat of the moment will probably burn you. It could get you fired. It could mean you never see your child again. Don't do it. Think.

I'm finding these days that anger is a choice. I don't have to go around with a sour attitude. I don't have to be overcome by rage. Author of the *Seven Habits of Highly Effective People*, Steven Covey, has said,

> " . . . it is the will that really makes effective self-management possible. It is the ability to make decisions and choices and to act in accordance with them. It is the ability to act rather than to be acted upon."

People say, "It made me angry." No. No-one can really *make* me angry. I decide. And with God's help I can control it.

If anyone doesn't believe me that it can be controlled, let me ask you this – have you ever been in an argument with someone at home where you're shouting and hot under the collar. Then the phone rings. What happens next? You've been yelling and screaming and you pick up the phone, now you talk really nicely to whoever so they can't see the steam coming out of the ears and your red hot angry little face. Hey presto! Instant change!

Ready for another fool test? Here goes:

> *"A fool shows his annoyance at once,*
> *but a prudent man overlooks an insult."* [56]

What you get upset over shows the depth of your character and how big you are on the inside. I want to learn to be less touchy. I'm definitely a work in progress, but positively, these days there are fewer things that I'm willing to argue about. Few things are worth dying in a ditch for and falling out over, whereas at times in the past I saw pretty much everything as life and death.

Shane Lynch used to be in one of the biggest boy bands of the 1990s, Boyzone. He publicly attributes most of the problems he had before becoming a believer in Christ to his temper. But speaking recently at my church about how knowing Jesus makes a difference Shane said, "I'm not the man I'm going to be, but I'm not the man I was."

We all know people who can't ignore *anything*; they'll gnaw any bone of contention thrown their way. The terrible shame is that Christians will fall out worse than those who don't know the Lord. Years ago, while in a police car, I actually came to blows with my best friend over a point of debate over church government! It's been said that a small pot boils quickly.

Hurricane

Denzel Washington appeared in the hit film, *Hurricane*. It's without doubt Washington's most impressive performance based on a real character who stood up for his innocence against terrible odds. I can also say that this movie had a very rare effect upon me, it made me blubber like a baby at a film for the first time in years (not very good for the street cred as I happened to be watching it in an aeroplane!).

It's the true story of how in the 1960s two black men shot and killed three people in a café. Rubin "Hurricane" Carter, a celebrated black boxer, was falsely charged and wrongly convicted in a highly publicised trial fuelled by intense racism. He maintained his innocence, studied and taught himself law inside. After serving nineteen years, Carter was released.

If anyone ever had a right to be an angry man, you'd think it would be Rubin Carter. But interviewed as a free man, Carter talked about his response to the injustice he has suffered. Was he bitter?

> "After all that's been said and done – the fact that the most productive years of my life, between the ages of twenty-nine and fifty, have been stolen; the fact that I was deprived of seeing my children grow up – wouldn't you think I would have a right to be bitter? Wouldn't anyone under those circumstances have a right to be bitter?
>
> If I have learned nothing else in my life, I've learned that bitterness only consumes the vessel that contains it. And for me to permit bitterness to control or to infect my life in any way whatsoever would be to allow those who imprisoned

me to take even more than the twenty-two years they've already taken. Now that would make me an accomplice to their crime." [57]

What does it take to get *you* angry? The wisest man that ever ruled Israel declared,

> *"A man's wisdom gives him patience;*
>   *it is to his glory to overlook an offence."* [58]

Maturity these days looks less like trying to appear holier than I am, as if I've got it all together. It's more about the ability to overlook it when someone says or does something that could hurt me. When I play it down, disregard it or shrug it off, I'm glorious. Because that's when I'm actually learning to become more like Jesus, following my Rabbi, mastering the art of living the full life. I'm being superhuman! Glorious, like my God.

> *"I will not carry out my fierce anger . . .*
> *For I am God, and not man –*
>   *the Holy One among you.*
>   *I will not come in wrath."* [59]

The Bible predicted and then described the attitude and demeanour of Jesus as he was crucified. Remember he had done nothing wrong.

> *"He was oppressed and afflicted,*
>   *yet he did not open his mouth;*

> he was led like a lamb to the slaughter,
>   and as a sheep before her shearers is silent,
>   so he did not open his mouth." [60]

Jesus was exhausted, brutalised, criticised, lied about, slandered, spat on, scorned, put down, and maligned. Yet he never fought back, spat back, kicked back or swore back. What a man!

The curse of the cross

The greatest curse in those days (this is what a Roman would do to another who carved up his chariot or insulted him in some way) was a rude gesture. Do this:

> Touch your forehead, then your stomach, then your left shoulder and then your right shoulder.

The sign of the cross said, "May you go to a cross!" There was nothing worse you could wish a person you were angry with.

People all round the world now sign themselves in prayer like that. Jesus has turned an angry curse into the place of greatest blessing for us. Maybe that's why I find it impossible to hold in my mind a picture of the cross, while at the same time remaining cross.

You and I can't choose our circumstances and challenges, but we can always choose our response. You do have a choice. Nothing can *make* you angry. You choose your response. When I'm getting irritated, and especially if I have a prior warning that I'm heading toward a situation where I'm likely to be, I try to remember to ask myself a question: "Is this worth giving up my happiness and peace for?"

In other words, "In the great scheme of things, is this really a big deal? Is it worth being upset over?" Some things aren't worth fighting for are they? Why win this battle and lose a friend?

I'm trying to analyse my anger a little more these days. To ask myself, "Why is this getting to me? Why am I so upset?" I find that anger is not itself the problem. It's the fizzing fuse leading to a bigger bomb. Anger is never the real problem. Anger is a warning light urgently flashing away to tell me there's a deeper issue that needs fixing inside. It's not the real problem, it's a symptom of something hidden.

A man went to confession and told the priest, "Father, forgive me, during the war I hid a refugee in my attic."

"Son, that was a wonderful thing, you saved his life."

"But father, I made him pay rent."

"That was not so nice, but you can surely be forgiven."

"Oh, thank you, father, but I have one more question."

"What is it, my son?"

"Do you think I have to tell him that the war is over?"

Are you holding someone in with your anger? The world has a lot of angry people in it. How about you? Maybe you feel angry because you're hurt. Hurt people hurt people. When you're physically, spiritually, or emotionally hurt you get angry. Emotional hurt causes anger. Perhaps you feel angry because you feel frustrated. Perhaps it's because you have to wait. Or things never seem to go quite as planned. Things don't seem to work (DIY doesn't DI for ME!). These things seem to come at us in a landslide and we have to somehow fight our way out.

Hurt people hurt people

From pastoral experience I think a lot of anger comes out of *insecurity*. Like an animal backed into a corner. You feel threatened, attacked as person because your position or self-image is challenged. Your self-worth is attacked, kindling the fire of anger.

A lot of times in a marriage or another relationship, you *think* you know what the problem is – you're angry. You think that's your problem. No. It seems to me you're probably insecure. Italian psychologist Alfred Adler (who coined the phrase, "inferiority complex") said, "All people with an overactive temper are just insecure."

I don't have to get angry. I can put that on my "Don't have to do" list. There's another way. A better way. The way of the full life.

I never lose my temper!

You might be thinking, "This isn't a problem for me because I never lose my temper." So you're keeping it then? What *do* you do with anger and frustration? Lots of people don't express it, they repress it. Pushing it down inside. That's called *somatising* – it means keeping it inside your body. Not a healthy option! If you don't talk it out, you take it out on your body, and that'll show up in all kinds of problems.

Anger is morally neutral. It's a normal response of your sympathetic nervous system to external stimuli. There are biochemical changes in your body when you push your anger down. It has been shown to increase the risk of atrial fibrillation (a heart condition). So what do you do instead of repress it?

Confess it

Admit your anger to God. It won't just get better, because,

> *"He who conceals his sins does not prosper,*
> *but whoever confesses and renounces them finds mercy."* [61]

Be honest with him in prayer, tell him exactly how you feel. You can tell him anything and never surprise him or shock him, because he knows it already! Confess for your benefit. Own up to anger, pain, a wounded heart. Then when you've got rid of that ugly junk, you're ready for God to fill you and give you the help you need.

As I reflect on the changes Jesus has brought about in my life, perhaps the greatest of them has been to help deal with my own anger. For years in the police I was an angry, violent man. I missed the violence of the police when I left to train for ministry, so much so that I took up rugby without any skill and no clue of the rules just so I could engage in some legal physical confrontation every now and then! Every house I lived in from eighteen to thirty-five years old had a hole in the door, or a rubbish bin that had been kicked to pieces in my rage.

Until just the other week in the middle of an enormous row (when the bin looked at me in a funny way and paid the price of defiance), I would have been able to say I'd changed a great deal. But like my friend Shane, I'm not the man I want to be, but I'm not the man I was either.

I am not perfect, but I am not as angry as I was. Jesus helps me by loving me lavishly and unconditionally throughout and dealing with the root problems. My Master, Jesus, is still at work on my heart. I don't have to be angry because Jesus heals my hurts by loving me with perfect love when I'm so much less than perfect. I am the apple of his eye. He is not fickle. He continually replaces hurt with his love, frustration with peace, insecurity with power. I don't feel threatened by situations, events or people that used to really get to me, because God got to me first.

How are you doing in this area?

Exercises

- "You can't stay in your corner of the Forest waiting for others to come to you. You have to go to them sometimes." That bit of wisdom comes from *Winnie the Pooh!* You may need to apologise to somebody. Acknowledge your imperfect response. "I'm sorry for my anger and harsh words." Tell them you want to change and ask them to pray that you'll be able to.

- Make a list of the situations you most often find cause you to become angry. Ask God to show you the deeper reason behind your reaction.

- In general, are you most likely to boil up so everyone knows, or outwardly appear calm while you somatise the hurt?

- Discuss the ideas in this chapter with a trusted friend. Ask them whether they have seen much evidence that this could be a problem for you. (Note I did say a *trusted* friend!)

- Do some vigorous exercise when you feel angry, it will use the hormone rush as the Maker intended and help you feel calmer. Activity neutralises the stress created by unexpressed anger.

I Don't Have to
Feel Guilty Any More

"Shame is the lie someone told you about yourself."
(Anais Nin)

> *"My guilt has overwhelmed me*
>   *like a burden too heavy to bear.*
> *My wounds fester and are loathsome*
>   *because of my sinful folly.*
> *I am bowed down and brought very low;*
>   *all day long I go about mourning.*
> *My back is filled with searing pain;*
>   *there is no health in my body.*
> *I am feeble and utterly crushed;*
>   *I groan in anguish of heart."*

(Psalm 38:4–8, NIV)

It's not a contender for happiest song of the year is it? But what's the reason? Why does he feel so weak and low that he goes on to talk about avoiding people, and them avoiding him? Why does he feel like someone with arrows sticking out of him? The answer is in verse 4:

> *"My guilt has overwhelmed me*
> *like a burden too heavy to bear."*

You could literally translate it like this, *"My guilt has covered over my head: heavy – and heavily weighing me down."* Guilt will do that to you. At times you can perhaps shake it off and put it behind you, but in the end, guilt weighs you down, shame holds you down, paralyses you and stops you moving on.

Ever felt weighed down by guilt? Guilty feelings are heavy stuff.

- Ever heard a little, familiar nagging whisper that calls you a fake? Coward? Dumbo? Fraud?
- Do you sometimes suspect that if people saw past the veneer and knew the real blemished you, no-one would want to know you?
- Ever thought that you just don't (and can't) measure up to some *really* good people you know are doing a better job at life in general – and being good in particular – than you?
- And what about God? The one who sees what is done in secret, who knows our thoughts as well as our words and actions. Ever felt God must be pretty disgusted when he looks at you? How could "the Holy One of Israel" accept *you*?

I've felt all those things. I've played all those tapes over and over in my head. I know what guilt can do, how it makes you feel sick, ties you down, presses you, discourages you. The weight of guilt caused by sin holds you under an invisible but arduous, smothering force. God seems a million miles away, if he really exists at all. No wonder people talk about the *gravity* of an offence. It gets you down.

I can't do what I want to do, I can't *be* who I want to be. I've become what I have done. It's not just that I have *done* something bad, I *am* bad.

One day the Master of the full life, Rabbi Jesus of Nazareth, wrapped up a tour and came back to his home town. Local boy makes good. Everyone loved his teaching, people flocked from all over to hear him. The people of his home village were the proudest. It was said that he spoke as one with authority. That meant this Teacher was looking at the Torah (the first five books of the Old Testament) in new ways and even bringing new applications. The crowds loved that! They'd travel miles on foot to hear someone with authority.

They loved all those exciting stories. They enjoyed the way he burst the bubbles of the self-righteous and rained on the parade of pompous experts in the law. He ran rings around their amateur probing with the questions he answered them with. Of course there were rumours of wonderful miracles that he'd performed in other places. What would he be able to do here? Playing at home. Everyone bought the T-shirt and key rings.

Ever wondered why so many stories in the gospels are about Jesus healing people from some kind of physical deformity? Part of the answer has to be because those events were so spectacular they stayed in the mind. Maybe they were recorded to show the power of God in Jesus. But I think there's another reason these stories were recorded. When we read about Jesus healing physical deformities isn't it also showing us how God can heal our invisible deformities? The scars, lumps and bumps in your soul. What if these healings show us how God might approach your heart, reshaping our deformities into places of healing and power?

Carried to Jesus

In Jesus' home town there lived a paralysed man. He couldn't move. This man had been on his back and pinned down a long time, but he had friends who believed in him, people who loved him. These friends carried him and brought him to Jesus. Maybe Jesus knew the man, after all, they'd been brought up in the same town.

Who knows whether this guy was a really good hearted man who'd never hurt anyone and now was suffering silently and with dignity? Who knows whether he had been school bully at Nazareth Primary School, and now he was cantankerous, angry and hate filled? Who knows whether he had sins that needed to be dealt with, and a weight of guilt holding him down?

Jesus knew. God knew. The prophet Samuel was told,

> "God judges persons differently than humans do. Men and women look at the face; God looks into the heart." [62]

You and I might see a man who couldn't move lying there paralysed and think God's first work needs to be to get him healed. That would certainly be the politically correct way to deal with this. Apparently Jesus saw something more, something needing urgent attention, something that had to be dealt with straight away. The man had something wrong with his heart. So Jesus went to work with a word.

"My friend, don't worry! Your sins are forgiven." [63]

It's been said that the heart of the human problem is the problem of the human heart. Jesus went straight to the heart of the man's problem. Whatever *he* might have thought his main difficulty was, Jesus knew that whether or not he felt guilty, he was guilty. He needed to know that his sins had been sent away – which is the literal sense of the Greek word used here – before he could get up and move on.

Anyone can end up paralysed by sin. By that I mean weighed down, unable to move, unable to go where we want or do what we want to do. You might look perfectly capable to others, but I have to tell you, you have a problem with your heart too and only Jesus Christ can fix it! He wants you to get up and move on into the plan he has for you. That's why he made sure you got a copy of this book. That was no accident.

How does that blanket of shame fall on us? It takes various forms.

Things we have done

This is the most obvious. We have all missed the mark. Not all guilt is bad, if it gets us to face the truth about ourselves. And it's not pretty. Billy Graham once said that he knew his own heart and that without God's restraining grace on his life he also knew there was not a sin known to humanity that he could not commit given the right (or rather the wrong) circumstances.

A carpet cleaning company came up with a great way to get new customers who had pets. To show potential customers their need for the service, the salesman made sure his appointment was booked for an evening so he could darken the room, before turning on a powerful black light. The black light caused urine crystals to glow brightly.

To the horror of the householder, every drop and dribble could be seen, not only on the carpet, but often on carpets, walls, furniture – even lamp shades.

The salesman said, "One woman told me, 'I'll never be comfortable in my home again.' Another begged, 'Please turn off the light, I can't bear to see anymore. I don't care what it costs. Please clean it up!' "

The mess was there all the time, invisible until the right light exposed it. It would have been cruel for the salesman to show customers the extent of their problem and then say, "Too bad," and walk away. He brought the light so they would know they desperately had to have the answer: his cleaning services.

I have experienced so many times when I've been reading the Bible or talking with someone, or been praying, God showing me a spot on my heart that needs to be clean. And then and there I have a choice. I can have an empty life or enjoy a full life. It depends what I do next.

Jesus saw the unseen and the unknown. Everyone knew about and could see the paralysed man's physical limitations, but Jesus could see beyond that. He knew that even a serious physical need was temporary and therefore not nearly as pressing as his spiritual need.

John chapter 3 tells us of two reactions people have when God shines his light on us, revealing stains and mess we have learned to live with and accept – or deny is even there.

> *"The light has come into the world, and people who do evil things are judged guilty because they love the dark more than the light. People who do evil hate the light and won't come to the light, because it clearly shows what they have done. But everyone who lives by the truth will come to the light, because they want others to know that God is really the one doing what they do."* [64]

In the same way, God shines the light on our hearts not just to convict us, make us feel guilty and leave us that way. He has a cleaning service to offer to those who want to live by the truth, when we face up to the fact of our sin and guilt, and ask Jesus to clean us up. As Christian communicator J. John wisely said, "Jesus didn't come to rub it *in*, he came to rub it *out!*"

God sends his Holy Spirit to convict us of our sins. It's the best thing he could do for us, not the worst. Conviction shows us where we're falling short and grieving the heart of God by choosing our own way that leads to death. By definition we are living in rebellion against him by choosing our own way, not his. We have to get real about that and get it sorted out.

In the Great Irish Famine of 1845 to 1847, up to one million people died and a similar number of people emigrated to the rest of Europe and the USA. Potato blight ranks as one of the most devastating diseases in human history, and it's not beaten yet. No potato is immune. The blight that struck the staple crop of those Irish farmers was a fungus-like organism called *phytophthora infestans*. What is particularly cruel is that it left the vegetables appearing on the outside to be large, firm, and hearty, but when it was cut open the potato revealed the blight had consumed it from the inside. The potato would be rotten, hollowed, soft and stinking to within a half inch of its outer skin. What looked so promising couldn't yield a single edible mouthful. The potatoes rotted from the inside out.

This is a picture of what the Bible means when it talks about sin and its effects. We may look fine (well more or less) on the outside. We're able to keep up appearances, but inside God knows we have this blight in our being that rots us from the inside out. Even if we look great on the outside, even if we are better than "bad people", our deep desires, our hidden hungers betray our true selves.

Paul the apostle summed up the problem writing to the church in Rome,

> *"For the good that I would I do not: but the evil which I would not, that I do."* [65]

Houston, we have a problem.

Imagine a farmer trying to pass off the spoiled spuds as, "No big deal?" The guilt of our sins really *is* a big deal to God. The outward appearance is deception. And there's no such thing as just a bit rotten. For example, we shade the truth, call it a white lie – and can't fully comprehend what a stench it is to God. There's no such thing as cheap grace – because our sins cost Jesus everything. Yours and mine.

I have to mention that amazing film *The Passion of the Christ* again, because Mel Gibson portrays this in a remarkable way by an amazing cameo performance. While Gibson's face never appears on screen, we do see his hands once. They are the ones that hold a spike and a hammer, as they nail Jesus to the cross.

Some people just never see their sin as being that serious. The prophet Jeremiah warns about such people:

> "... *they have no shame. They don't even know how to blush. There's no hope for them. They've hit bottom and there's no getting up.*" [66]

To be proud enough with how you are that you feel no shame over your sin is perhaps the greatest sin of all. It's said that when Goering was on trial at Nuremburg, listening to the charges being read out against him, he leaned across to a co-accused and said, "One day they'll build monuments to us."

We once looked into buying a house that looked great to us, but a survey soon found hidden structural problems. The worst thing we can do with guilt over sin we have committed is to paper over it or deny it. The best thing God can do for a stained heart is shine his light on it.

Things we have not done

Here's the next blanket of guilt that weighs people down. Most of us think that if we can scrape through a day or even a life without committing *too many* sins, or if we can compare ourselves with others and find our tally is short in comparison to theirs, then we're doing okay. But the Bible makes it clear that it's not just the things we have done that can cause us problems, we can *not* do some things and have guilt stains in need of cleaning up.

Johnny Cash wrote a great song that talks about the day of Jesus' return, it's called, "The Man Comes Around".

There's a man goin' 'round takin' names.
An' he decides who to free and who to blame.
Everybody won't be treated all the same.
There'll be a golden ladder reaching down.
When the man comes around.

The hairs on your arm will stand up.
At the terror in each sip and in each sup.
For you partake of that last offered cup,
Or disappear into the potter's ground.
When the man comes around.

Till Armageddon, no Shalam, no Shalom.
Then the father hen will call his chickens home.
The wise men will bow down before the throne.
And at his feet they'll cast their golden crown.
When the man comes around.

Whoever is unjust, let him be unjust still.
Whoever is righteous, let him be righteous still.
Whoever is filthy, let him be filthy still.
Listen to the words long written down,
When the man comes around.

One day Jesus says there's a day coming when he will line up a group of people who really will think they've done a pretty good job at life, and he'll face them with the truth.

> " 'I was hungry and you gave me no meal, I was thirsty and you gave me no drink, I was homeless and you gave me no bed, I was shivering and you gave me no clothes, Sick and in prison, and you never visited.' Then [they] are going to say, 'Master, what are you talking about? When did we ever see you hungry or thirsty or homeless or shivering or sick or in prison and didn't help?'
>
> He will answer them, 'I'm telling the solemn truth: Whenever you failed to do one of these things to someone who was being overlooked or ignored, that was me – you failed to do it to me.' Then [they] will be herded to their eternal doom . . . " [67]

Woah! Eternal doom doesn't sound too good to me. "But I haven't done anything!" Exactly! Here's God's judgment on things we *haven't* done, sins of omission rather than sins of commission. For anyone who went through the last few pages thinking to yourself, "Well I haven't done many bad things," the Bible's question seems to be, "How many good things should you have done, and didn't?"

The book of James puts it more bluntly than I find comfortable,

> " . . . the person who does not do the good he knows he should do is guilty of sin." [68]

A quick look around my house reminds me of the modern obsession with germ-free living. Those insidious, invisible bugs! Hidden in our hearts are the attitudes that produce avarice, deceit, and violation of our promises to God and to one another.

We need God's grace to cleanse us from the ease with which we notice the sins of others, finding ways to criticise. Our tongues become weapons rather than instruments of healing. We are easily angered but slow to forgive. We speak without listening and pretend to listen without hearing. We are more critical than helpful toward the poor in our midst. Sounds like this blanket of guilt gets heavier and heavier. And there's another layer to weigh us down.

Things we have not done well enough

We sometimes call this kind of guilt regret, or recrimination (which literally means "calling the crime to mind again"). Over and over we hear the internal voice that slates us for not being a "good enough" parent. However old we are we can't shake off the chastisement of not being a "good enough" child for *our* parents. There's the guilt of missed opportunities, misplaced priorities and misunderstood grace.

People feel guilt because they're out of work, or because their nose is too big and their legs too skinny. Ever heard that "not good enough" call? Sometimes it's fuzzy and undefined. But it lurks to weigh you down and trip you up.

- *You can never live up to your father's ideal.*
- *You're condemned to never quite finish a project because it's not perfect yet.*
- *You're not good looking enough, or bright enough.*
- *The things you said mean they can never forgive you or trust you again.*
- *The things you did mean you should never trust yourself.*
- *Now you've really blown it.*
- *You're too tall.*

- *You're not tall enough to make the team.*
- *You're a terrible husband.*
- *You can't ever really be happy because you know if you're going to be really spiritual you have to show God how sorry you are for being a miserable offender.*
- *And if anyone ever got to see the **real** you, they'd spit in your face and then run a mile.*

Lynne Truss' best seller, *Eats, Shoots and Leaves*, is subtitled, *"The zero tolerance guide to punctuation."* Some people have ended up so bound up in guilt-driven perfectionism they have zero tolerance for little slips or flaws or accidents. They go crazy if they make a common mistake like losing their car keys. It's just further proof for them that they are useless. Someone else's minor weakness is huge to you, it's as bad for you to forget to write as it is for someone else to write hate mail.

You remember the day as the one when you lost your temper, not as the day when you all went for a walk by the sea, because bad memories block out the good times for you.

You don't make decisions because you're afraid to make the wrong one.

When all you see is faults in yourself, chances are that's what you'll see in others, like the woman who said to her husband at a party, "you'd better not have any more drinks, you're starting to look blurred already."

Journalist Sydney Harris wrote, "Many people feel 'guilty' about things they shouldn't feel guilty about, in order to shut out feelings of guilt about things they should feel guilty about."

So, three layers of guilt that can pin us down and suffocate and paralyse us.

- *Things we have done.*
- *Things we have not done.*
- *Things we have not done well enough.*

What can lift the blankets of shame?

Let me show you two phrases from the Bible, and then tell you what I think is remarkable about them.

- *"I'm ... Public Sinner Number One."* [69]
- *"My conscience is clear."* [70]

The amazing thing? *The same person said them.* They came out of the same mouth. The apostle Paul knew what it was to be heartbroken by his sin, failure and guilt. He had persecuted Christians, thrown them in jail and been involved in their deaths. He wasn't denying what he'd done, rationalising it or comparing it with others so as to try to get himself off the hook. None of that would work anyway.

But Paul also knew what it was to have his conscience cleansed.

Nothing you can buy or do can cleanse a guilty conscience. The writer to the Hebrews encourages,

> *"Let us come near to God ... with **hearts that have been purified from a guilty conscience ...**"* [71]

We can "Domestos" germs away from us and still find ourselves full of a dirty mess, because we've allowed our inner selves to be corrupted and made unclean. Nothing under the kitchen counter can help us get clean enough. There's only one product available that works to get rid of these stains, visible and invisible. The same writer tells us that Jesus has opened up a new way for us. A divine exchange is freely offered; his spot-lessness for our stains.

We don't have to beat ourselves up any more. Because Jesus was beaten for our sins, we don't have to feel guilty any more. Because the innocent Son of God has taken the rap, we don't have to live up to impossible standards any more. Just accept the words that raise us from the stifling paralysis of guilt. The words of Jesus to this paralysed man on the mat, who is a picture of us in our helplessness to struggle free of our guilt, addressing his real and most serious problem.

- *"Friend"* – you need a friend when you're feeling guilty, and Jesus is the one who sticks closer than a brother.
- *"Don't worry ... your sins"* be they many or few, gross or minor, things we have done, things we have not done, things we have not done well enough...
- *"are forgiven."* So throw off the blanket and dance!

A little boy was visiting his grandparents and given a catapult to play with. He practised in the woods, but he could never hit his target. As he came back to Grandma's back yard, he saw her pet duck. Just out of impulse he took aim and let fly. The stone hit and the duck fell dead. The boy panicked. Desperately he hid the dead duck in the wood pile, only to look up and see his sister watching. Sally had seen it all, but she said nothing.

After lunch that day, Grandma said, "Sally, let's wash the dishes."

But Sally said, "Johnny told me he wanted to help in the kitchen today. Didn't you, Johnny?" And she whispered to him, "Remember the duck!" So Johnny did the dishes.

Later Grandpa asked if the children wanted to go fishing. Grandma said, "I'm sorry, but I need Sally to help make supper."

Sally smiled and said, "That's all taken care of. Johnny wants to do it."

Again she whispered, "Remember the duck." Johnny stayed while Sally went fishing.

After several days of Johnny doing both his chores and Sally's, finally he couldn't stand it. He confessed to Grandma that he'd killed the duck. "I know, Johnny," she said, giving him a hug. "I was standing at the window and saw the whole thing. Because I love you, I forgave you. I was just wondering how long you would let Sally make a slave of you." [72]

Believe and receive

If you're struggling with feelings of guilt, it's because you have not believed or actually personally *received* what Jesus has said in the Bible. I have done whatever I can throughout the book to help so that now you can see that his way really is the best way to live. This important area needs to be dealt with so you can walk fully in the new life of following the Master.

- Your sins are not too big to be unforgivable.
- Your sins are not too small to matter.

But you do not have to be a slave any more, because Jesus saw the whole thing and he's forgiven you already.

We know that the worst thing that can happen to someone who sins or commits a crime would be that they receive the death penalty. Now the one who is most qualified to judge us has walked across the courtroom, stood beside us in the dock and taken the maximum penalty, he paid it himself for us.

Here's yet another police story. Two not very bright men were on trial for armed robbery at Manchester Crown Court. A witness took the oath, the prosecuting barrister then asked, "You were at the scene when the robbery took place?"

"Yes."

"And you saw a blue car leaving at a high rate of speed?"

"Yes."

"And did you observe the occupants of that car?"

"Yes, two men."

"And are those two men present in court today?"

At this point the two defendants raised their hands.

Friend, don't worry! Your sins are forgiven!

Have you held your hands up, admitted yours sins, so you can receive that forgiveness? That's what gives the chief of sinners a clear conscience. It's God's antidote to guilt – and it's big enough to cover the sins of the whole world.

It comes freely and fully from God who promises: *"Though your sins are like scarlet, they shall be as white as snow..."*[73] It's offered to people who think they're already good enough, and received by those who know they are not. We can allow God to cleanse us of our sin and shame. We can bring our need to the Lord and allow our lives to be made whole, clean and new. What a gift. The blight of our sins has been eradicated.

We simply have to accept this gift of love and grace, given by a God who contrasts his kind of forgiveness with what we mortals stingily and grudgingly try to pass off as the same thing when he says, *"I will forgive* [your] *wickedness and will remember* [your] *sins no more."* [74] Put your name in there now and claim that amazing promise of the Bible.

Read on through the Bible and underline passages like this and you will begin to *feel* forgiven, I guarantee it. But the great thing for me is that this unconditional love of God is not even dependent on my feelings. It's a fact.

The apostle John (he preferred to be known as 'the one Jesus loves') wrote,

> *"If we say that we have no sin, we deceive ourselves, and there is no truth in us. But if we confess our sins to God, he will keep his promise . . . and* **will** *forgive us our sins and purify us from all our wrongdoing."* [75]

The word for "purify" there is what we get "catharsis" from. It's cathartic, a power-blasting. That's what God's forgiveness is like. Total.

A friend of mine owns vast industrial chicken sheds. If you ever want to see a mess, visit on a busy day. But when they have cleaned up in there with the industrial sprayers, you'd be stunned how clean it all looks. Literally spotless. There's no point trying to hide our sins from God. He sees them all the time, but he waits for us to point them out to him so he can clean them, and forever there will be no trace.

So on those days when I don't feel forgiven I need to trust that I am declared not guilty, acquitted, cleansed and set free; to shake off the blanket of guilt, pick up my mat and dance! I won't have to focus on my faults, failures, weaknesses and "cannots" any more, because God doesn't look at them. I am a work in progress headed toward a perfect day, until then I'll hold my head high. I can accept myself because I am accepted. Made fully acceptable.

Why not get somewhere quiet and invite God's presence. He'll send Jesus. You can know him.

Then because you can know him, you can talk to him and he will talk with you. You won't know much soul loneliness from then on. Tell him what's on your mind and heart. Invite him to shine the searchlight of his love there.

You can pray something along these lines, it's not the words that matter:

> "Lord, you are here now, and you call me your friend.
> You have seen my sins.
> Please clean them.
> You died on a cross so now I can live.
> You took the curse so I can know the blessing.
> You gave your life so I don't have to taste death.
> Please lift the blanket of guilt and shame.
> I hear you say, 'Your sins are forgiven, past, present
>   and future.'
> Things I have done.
> Things I have not done.
> Things I have not done well enough.
> I believe you love me and receive you as my friend
>   to lead me and my Lord to guide me.
> Thank you.
> Shape me and mould me to be what you want.
> I hear you say, 'Pick up your mat and walk.'
> I am forgiven.

My conscience is clear.
Thank you that I do not have to feel guilty,
  because I can walk into the future with you
  now and forever – you have set me free!"

Notes

1. John 10:10 (*The Message*).
2. Hebrews 13:5 (NKJV).
3. 1 Peter 5:7 (NKJV).
4. Zig Ziglar.
5. Matthew 17:20 (NKJV, emphasis added).
6. Luke 14:28–30 (CEV).
7. Luke 14:18–20 (CEV).
8. Stacey Padrick, *Living with Mystery* (Bethany House, 2001).
9. Isaiah 55:2 (NIV).
10. New Living Translation.
11. Deuteronomy 20:9 (GNB, emphasis added).
12. "Does Rejection Hurt?", Naomi I. Eisenberger, Matthew D. Leiberman, and Kipling D. Williams, *Science*, 10 October 2003, 302:290–292.
13. *Journal of Personality and Social Psychology*, 2001, 201:1058–1069.
14. John 1:10 (NIV).
15. Mark 10:33–34 (NKJV).
16. John 15:18–20 (NKJV).
17. Romans 12:18 (NIV).
18. Matthew 10:11–12 (GNB).
19. Dale Carnegie, *How to Win Friends and Influence People*, Vermilion, 1990.
20. Matthew 10:14 (CEV).
21. Galatians 1:10 (NIV).
22. From Matthew 10:16.
23. Flavius Josephus, *Antiquities of the Jews*, Book VI, ch. 7.
24. Mark 8:31–33 (*The Message*).
25. Mark 8:31 (CEV).
26. Johann Wolfgang Von Goethe.

27. Matthew 20:16 (NIV).
28. Matthew 6:33 (KJV).
29. 2 Corinthians 9:8 (NIV).
30. 3 John 2 (NKJV, emphasis added).
31. Ecclesiastes 5:13 (NIV).
32. Ecclesiastes 11:1 (NKJV).
33. *The Message.*
34. Joshua 7:1–25.
35. Malachi 3:10.
36. Look at 2 Corinthians 8:2.
37. 2 Corinthians 8:5 (NIV).
38. Luke 12:34 (NKJV).
39. 2 Corinthians 9:8 (NIV).
40. I believe this story was originally told by W. Somerset Maugham.
41. Paraphrase of Ecclesiastes 8:8.
42. *Stop All the Clocks* by W.H. Auden.
43. 1 Corinthians 15:26.
44. Matthew 7:13.
45. John 10:18 (NKJV).
46. Revelation 1:18.
47. Frederick Buechner.
48. Richard L. Pratt, Jr, *He Gave Us Stories* (P & R Publishing, 1990).
49. Proverbs 27:6 (NIV).
50. Proverbs 14:29 (NIV).
51. Proverbs 11:29 (LB).
52. Proverbs 21:23 (NIV).
53. Proverbs 15:1 (*The Message*, emphasis added).
54. Matthew 11:29 (NIV).
55. Proverbs 29:11 (NIV).
56. Proverbs 12:16 (NIV).
57. James S. Hirsch, *Hurricane: The Miraculous Journey of Rubin Carter* (Fourth Estate Ltd, 2000).
58. Proverbs 19:11 (NIV).
59. Hosea 11:9 (NIV).
60. Isaiah 53:7 (NIV).
61. Proverbs 28:13 (NIV).
62. 1 Samuel 16:7 (*The Message*).
63. Matthew 9:2 (CEV).
64. John 3:19–21 (CEV).
65. Romans 7:19 (KJV).

66. Jeremiah 6:15 (*The Message*).
67. Matthew 25:42–46 (*The Message*).
68. James 4:17 (GNB).
69. From 1 Timothy 1:15 (*The Message*).
70. 1 Corinthians 4:4 (NIV).
71. Hebrews 10:22 (GNB).
72. From *Will Daylight Come?* by Richard Hoefler, quoted at www.inhis.com/Stories/Story.asp?id=1030.
73. Isaiah 1:18 (NIV).
74. Jeremiah 31:34 (NIV).
75. 1 John 1:8–9 (GNB emphasis added).

Contact Anthony Delaney

If you would like information about Anthony's upcoming speaking engagements or consulting services for your church, business or organisation, please send your name, address, and organisation details to:

Anthony Delaney
L1FE
The Wheelhouse
East Lane
West Horsley
Surrey
KT24 6LQ

Tel: +44 (0)1483 281898
Email: enquiry@l1fe.org

We hope you enjoyed reading this New Wine book.
For details of other New Wine books
and a range of 2,000 titles from other
Word and Spirit publishers visit our website:
www.newwineministries.co.uk